SCOTLAND'S SHAME

Scotland's Shame

WHY LOCKERBIE STILL MATTERS

John Ashton

BIRLINN

First published in 2013 by
Birlinn Limited
West Newington House
10 Newington Road
Edinburgh
EH9 1QS

www.birlinn.co.uk

ISBN-13: 978 1 78027 167 5

British Library Cataloguing-in-Publication Data
A catalogue record for this book is available from the
British Library

Set in Sabon at Birlinn

Printed and bound by Grafica Veneta
www.graficaveneta.com

Contents

Acknowledgements

Having spent two and a half years writing *Megrahi: You Are My Jury*, I never imagined that I would write another book about Lockerbie. The fact that I have is down to Hugh Andrew and his colleagues at Birlinn, who understand the importance of the story and its particular importance to Scotland. My sincere thanks to them, especially Tom Johnstone for his editorial guidance and Jan Rutherford for coordinating the book's publicity. I'm also grateful to Professor Bob Black, Robert Forrester, Tony Kelly, Morag Kerr, Simon McKay, Iain McKie and Robert Parry for their editorial advice and moral support. Dr Jim Swire has done more than anyone to keep the Lockerbie issue alive and I'm very honoured that he has written the book's foreword. My wife Anja uttered not a whisper of protest when I told her that I wanted to write a new book, and she and our son Paolo have cheered me on throughout.

Foreword
by Jim Swire

'Love one another with a pure heart fervently, see
that ye love one another.'
Peter 1:22 and Samuel Sebastian Wesley (1810-1876)

When I was a boy, some 70 years ago, I remember being sent
away from my much loved home in the Isle of Skye, where
our daughter Flora's ashes now lie buried, to go to boarding
school in Oxford. I dreaded those journeys; but when I was
singing in the school choir there as a boy treble, a favourite
hymn was Samuel Wesley's anthem which, to glorious music,
contains the command, 'Love one another with a pure heart
fervently, see that ye love one another.'

Through my long life it has often proved hard to follow
that command to love one another, and I have often been a
miserable failure at it, even in loving my own family as they
deserved at times. But the greatest tests have come since our
deeply loved elder daughter Flora was slaughtered, a day short
of her twenty-fourth birthday, along with 269 others, in the
Lockerbie atrocity of 1988. She was a beautiful, ebullient
young medical student, so bright that she had volunteered
temporarily to suspend her medical studies in Nottingham
to do a research project at the country's premier neurological
institute in Queen's Square, London. There she met a young
American doctor who became her boyfriend. It was to him in
Boston that she wanted to fly for Christmas 1988 after having
asked her mum if it was OK for her to be away from the family
for Christmas. How hard it is: if we had only said no . . . we
would still have our Flora with us, and I would not be writing
this now.

During the painful task of clearing out her London room
after her death, we found on her desk a letter from Cambridge,

my old university, accepting her to continue her studies there. We knew this meant we would have heard her excited voice, probably on Christmas Day, telling of her safe arrival and her acceptance by Cambridge. But it was never to be.

Now that John Ashton and so many others have been able to make it plain that the 'official version' of the Libyan Abdel-baset al-Megrahi's guilt cannot be true, it has become increasingly difficult not to despise those who still try to defend the indefensible. Most of them do this out of ignorance, but some because they are told to do so, some to enhance their careers, some to conceal their own shame, some to seek greater power, some to make money, others because they genuinely see it as their duty to toe the official line.

When John Ashton's second Lockerbie book, *Megrahi: You Are My Jury* was published in Edinburgh, an announcement from 10 Downing Street, which had not had time to study its contents, early that same morning condemned the book as an insult to the relatives. Now that fifteen months have gone by, there can be no excuse for the government's failing to have studied afresh the origins of the murder of so great a number of innocent citizens, so clearly set out by Ashton. The failure to protect our families and the denial of the truth are the real insults for the relatives.

This, Ashton's third Lockerbie book, shows that terrible mistakes have been made, and there are hints of something more sinister than simple human error. For us, being denied the truth has become the norm, but Ashton's work is fresh and closely reasoned from his vantage point in possession of almost all the evidence available to both prosecution and defence. It seems that our own and certain other governments are deliberately concealing the truth from us. This is both wrong and futile, for Article 2 of the European Convention on Human Rights enshrines our absolute right to know the truth about the deaths and the failure to protect our families. The longer that government refuses to reveal all it really knows of the truth, the more certain it is that the Supreme Court or the European Court of Human Rights will have to intervene. There will be no mercy at the bar of history.

It has never been the aim of the Lockerbie victims' relatives' group, UK Families-Flight 103, to attack those who made mistakes; rather we seek ways to ensure that our courts shall function transparently and fairly in future. How much better that that the investigation and correction of what has gone wrong should come from within our own borders.

In 1990 the UK relatives were summoned to the US embassy in London to hear the findings of President George Bush senior's Commission on Aviation Security and Terrorism. It seemed to be a review of how the US would fight terrorism in future – a foretaste perhaps of how the American 'war on terror' would later impact on all our lives. It sought to reassure us that there had been no sinister explanation as to why the Lockerbie aircraft had only been two-thirds full in the week before Christmas and how it came to be that some of our families had been told there were no seats to the US that week, only to be offered seats in the last few days before the flight, on the Lockerbie aircraft Pan Am 103.

However, one of our number, Martin Cadman, who had lost a son, was taken aside in the embassy by a member of the Commission and told quietly, 'Your government and ours know exactly what happened, but they are never going to tell.'

Even the least imaginative among us might from then on have wondered, was this atrocity some incident in a great game of international politics, in which individuals and truth may be sacrificed for the perceived national interests of a whole country?

After all, five months before Lockerbie, a US missile cruiser, the USS *Vincennes*, had shot down an Iranian airbus killing 290 innocent people, and then the United States had awarded a medal to her captain and meritorious service ribbons to her crew. The Iranians had naturally bayed for revenge, an eye for an eye; was Lockerbie that revenge? If so was it in any sense 'facilitated' to avoid inevitable confrontation with Iran? What a terrible possibility; but fear of such a horror becoming public could explain the effort still ongoing by governments to obstruct the truth. We do know it was initially a given in intelligence and civil aviation circles that Lockerbie was indeed Iran's revenge, so why was no coherent move apparently made to prevent it?

In 1991 Scotland and America decided to issue indictments against Megrahi and his fellow Libyan, Lamin Fhimah, claiming they had been agents working in Malta to get a Libyan-provided IED (bomb) aboard the Lockerbie flight by a circuitous route involving Frankfurt airport. Within days of the indictments against the two Libyans, American and UK hostages started to be returned to freedom by the Iranian-backed groups such as Hezbollah who had been holding them. One of the first two to be released was Britain's Terry Waite.

The hostage issue was an enduring obsession for the Reagan and Bush administrations and had given rise to the disastrous and illegal Iran-Contra operation a few years earlier. It was perhaps not surprising that some of us began to wonder just what the driving forces behind the evolution of the Lockerbie investigation might be.

Then in 1998, following a meeting of Robin Cook, UK Foreign Secretary, with us, the UK relatives, in Edinburgh, and strengthened by the support of Nelson Mandela and American money under President Clinton, an arrangement was signed between the UK and Dutch Governments to allow a trial of the two accused Libyans in a 'Scottish enclave' within Holland.

Ever since the issue of the indictments in 1991, I had repeatedly visited Colonel Gadafy in Tripoli, slowly losing my fear of him and begging him to allow his two citizens to attend for trial under Scots law, which at that time I believed would offer a fair trial. During this time I also came to meet, liaise with and respect Professor Robert Black QC. A native of Lockerbie himself, and emeritus professor of Scots law at Edinburgh University, it was he who had defined the concept of a Scottish court sitting in a neutral country to try the two accused. His concept was modified before the court could sit in such a way that there was to be no jury, and the panel of judges was to be Scottish, not international.

Nelson Mandela had warned in Edinburgh that 'No one country should be complainant, prosecutor and judge.' But Scotland now became all three.

Along with one other member of the group, Reverend John Mosey, who had also lost a daughter, Helga, on the plane, and who has become a very dear friend, we attended throughout the Zeist trial of the two Libyans and their first appeal. It was a surreal experience. First we witnessed the grooming of US relatives by members of the prosecution team most evenings, and then much of the evidence seemed to be coherent but to point to a Syrian-based terror group, the PFLP-GC, which was closely associated with Iran, and not towards Malta and Megrahi.

Upon hearing the Zeist verdict, at first we felt very isolated in our realisation that the trial did not seem to have delivered justice; but then Professor Black, despite being the main originator of the concept of a neutral country trial and a leading upholder of Scottish justice, was amongst the first to publish warnings that the trial had not been a valid one under Scots law. In that he was joined by Professor Hans Köchler of Vienna, UN special observer at the trial, who found that the proceedings were not recognisable as justice. A host of others began to cry foul.

Apart from the unstinting love and support of my wife Jane, key among the new friends made during the first years of torture were the other members of our group, UK Families-Flight 103. Skillfully run by Jean Berkley and her husband Barrie, who had lost their son Alistair, the group has supported its members and sought truth and justice resolutely through-out all this time, often guided by solicitor Gareth Peirce, and despite the repeated insults we suffered just because we could not accept the trial's verdict. The group has also always tried to find ways by which we could give something back to the world for the privilege of having shared some of our lives with those who died: how could we force something good out of something as savage and evil as this atrocity?

I had refused an opportunity to meet the two accused on one of my visits to urge Colonel Gaddafi to allow them to attend for trial. However, on observing them in court and lis-tening to the evidence, it became increasingly clear that they might not after all be guilty. After the trial and during frequent interactions with solicitor Tony Kelly, who took over the de-fence team in 2005, it also became clear that those who knew Megrahi best were not simply defending a client but genuinely believed in his innocence. This, combined with news of his positive interactions with his fellow prisoners and my own growing certainty of his innocence, led me to go to see him in Greenock prison. Despite the comments of one Lord Advocate that I must be suffering from Stockholm syndrome, a friend-ship developed which, although it could not be as close as that of John Ashton who saw him often, became increasingly important to both of us.

I shall never forget my last visit to him as he lay dying and in great pain in Tripoli. He was still able between gasps for breath to show his concern that certain documents which he had set aside for me concerning his innocence should reach me safely after his death, which they did and have been lodged with John Ashton for safe keeping. He also repeated his con-cern that the curse of being 'the bomber's family' should be lifted from the shoulders of his wife Aisha and the children af-ter he had gone. I treasure having had the privilege of sharing that friendship and know that he too valued it, perhaps espe-cially when he was still in prison and unable to see his family.

I do not know if even compassion could have empowered such a friendship for me without the knowledge of his innocence. Certainly I could not have begged Kenny MacAskill to allow the man I had come to know as Baset to go home had I still thought he was guilty. Because some others among us relatives still believed he was involved, it was a tough call to make that plea to MacAskill in the presence of one or two of them, although we knew that if he was to go home on the basis of Scotland's provision for compassionate release, there was no obligation to stop his appeal. I leave the assessment of why Baset did withdraw his appeal to John Ashton's book. Although I have no idea whether my plea made any difference to MacAskill's decision, it was a privilege to be given the opportunity to make it, and I have felt some shame at the appalling and ill-informed ranting against our country and the Justice Secretary which followed Baset's release.

That decision to use compassionate release is for me one aspect of this dreadful case about which I think Scotland should be proud, even though I cannot be sure why Baset did stop his appeal when he did not have to. The appeal would not block his release, it could have continued with him in Tripoli. Perhaps things would have gone worse for him and his family in Tripoli if his country had told him to stop the appeal as well as to come home. Knowing all we now know of the evidence that was about to be led in that appeal, it must have been a huge relief to the Crown Office that the snail's pace of their conduct of that second appeal had allowed Baset's cancer to catch up with him. I'll guess that the single malts were out that evening in Chambers Street, but you won't find such speculation as that in Ashton's book.

It may be that the forming of this friendship is something which is intrinsically good emerging from the great evil of the atrocity. It certainly was for us both.

The doctrine of attempting to love our fellow humans is not restricted to those who believe in a God. Believers of every hue, agnostics and atheists, we all share the human predicament and we can all see the human need for help; but in no way does such an awareness free any of us from the duty of identifying wrongdoers and of sentencing them if caught, according to a tariff of punishments established by precedent and consent within the criminal law of our communities. In civilised communities justice is the surrogate for the lust for revenge, that destructive passion, which is latent in us all, and which was certainly the motive for Lockerbie.

Provided that our justice system remains objective and free from extrinsic interference it is the best route to the management of offenders, but it is also dependent upon the integrity with which the evidence is assembled, and the sharing of all the available relevant evidence for use by both prosecution and defence.

Thank God we still have some space for compassion in our justice system in Scotland, and no death penalty, so that the consequences of injustice can be diminished sometimes. But the consequences of a miscarriage of justice also ensure that the real perpetrators of a crime will be free to strike again, and other potential killers may be emboldened.

As Juvenal asked some 2,000 years ago, 'Sed quis custodiet ipsos custodes?' (who guards the guardians?). The refusal to date of the Scottish Government to enquire into the behaviour of their own Crown Office or individuals involved in the case, even though they unquestionably have the powers to do so, and have the findings of their Scottish Criminal Cases Review Commission to guide them, as well as John Ashton's careful analysis, is discouraging.

Scottish justice survived the Act of Union with England with its independence intact: perhaps since then it has been a talisman of Scotland's reputation as an independent nation capable of running its own affairs. If that is so, Scotland – my country – would do well to address the apparent problem of the impenetrable arrogance of her prosecuting authorities that seem to have blighted her justice system ever since it became clear that the Lockerbie trial had been defective.

The problem must be addressed, and done so with transparency, for it will not just go away. It is best addressed from within Scotland herself and may well be a factor which will block independence until it is resolved, for an independent community with an obscured and mistrusted justice system can never be a healthy community. We would wish healing, not harm, for Scotland and all her people, but the arrogant refusal to consider fault has dragged on so long and is so great a threat now to her reputation in the world that the cure is not likely to be found within the timescale now scheduled for the independence debate. It is to be hoped that the refusal of the current Scottish government to intervene with an independent inquiry, despite clearly having the powers required to do so, is not driven by motives of party advantage. The terrible events of Lockerbie deserve far greater respect than that.

Jim Swire, 9 May 2013.

Preface

Lockerbie does not shame the Scottish people, rather it shames their two most powerful institutions: the criminal justice system and the Scottish government.

It is now 25 years since Pan Am flight 103 crashed on to the Dumfriesshire town and 12 years since Abdelbaset al-Megrahi was convicted of the bombing. This book will argue that the case has become the biggest scandal of the country's post-devolution era. This is not because the terminally ill Libyan was released from prison, but because he should never have been charged with the murders and, still less, convicted. As a consequence of these follies the perpetrators of Europe's worst terrorist attack went free, the 270 Lockerbie victims and their relatives were denied justice and the Libyan people were forced to endure years of devastating economic sanctions. The scandal happened because the criminal justice system failed in its most basic duties, and it has intensified because the government has continually looked the other way.

Last year my book *Megrahi: You Are My Jury* revealed crucial evidence that the Crown had failed to disclose to Megrahi's defence team. Those, like Dr Jim Swire, who care about justice, were outraged, while the supposed guardians of justice ignored or condemned the book. This much shorter work is less about the fine detail of the case and more about what has gone wrong.

It is not, of course, an issue that directly affects the public's well-being, yet many people in Scotland and beyond are concerned. That is why Megrahi received a constant stream of supportive letters and why hundreds of people will turn up to hear Dr Swire speak. It matters to them because justice matters, and in this case, justice miscarried spectacularly. It also matters because the institutions that are supposed to safeguard justice are in denial about their failure.

John Ashton, August 2013.

Flawed Charges 1

At 19.03 on Wednesday 21 December 1988, Pan Am flight PA103 broke apart over the Scottish Borders. Within minutes all 259 passengers and crew were dead, along with 11 residents of Lockerbie. The wreckage spread over 845 square miles east of the town. Forensic investigators established within days that an explosion had occurred in the forward left baggage hold. Hundreds of police officers, military personnel and volunteer searchers combed the vast crime scene for clues, while detectives investigated in Europe, the US, the Middle East, West Africa and beyond.

Almost three years later, on 14 November 1991, Scotland's chief prosecutor, the Lord Advocate Lord Fraser of Carmyllie, and the US acting Attorney General, William Barr, simultaneously announced charges against two Libyans: Abdelbaset al-Megrahi and Lamin Fhimah. The media were briefed that the bombing was Colonel Gadafy's revenge for the 1986 US air raids on Libya.

The case appeared strong. It was alleged that on the morning of the bombing the two men placed an unaccompanied brown Samsonite suitcase on Air Malta flight KM180 from Malta to Frankfurt. The suitcase contained a bomb concealed within a Toshiba radio-cassette player and was said to be labelled for New York on PA103. At Frankfurt it was supposedly transferred to a Pan Am feeder flight, PA103A, to London Heathrow, and at Heathrow to PA103.

The suitcase was packed with clothes that Megrahi had allegedly bought in Malta on 7 December. It was claimed that he took the case from Libya to Malta on 20 December, while travelling on a coded passport under the name of Ahmed Khalifa Abdusamad. The following morning he flew

1

back to Libya on a Libyan Arab Airlines (LAA) flight, which checked-in shortly before KM180, and somehow, with Fhimah's help, managed to smuggle the suitcase into KM180's baggage hold.

Police enquiries in Malta traced bomb-damaged clothes to a small shop called Mary's House in the town of Sliema. Miraculously, shopkeeper Tony Gauci remembered selling the clothes to an oddly behaved man shortly before the Lockerbie bombing. Later to become the star witness against Megrahi, Gauci said the mystery customer was Libyan. He couldn't recall the date of the purchase, but said it was midweek and that his younger brother Paul, who usually worked in the shop, was at home watching football on TV. Another important clue was a blast-damaged pair of brown checked trousers found at the crash site, which were made by a Maltese company, Yorkie Clothing. When the police cross-checked an order number printed on a pocket with the company's order book, they discovered that the trousers had been delivered to the shop on 18 November 1988. When shown the TV schedules, Paul narrowed down the date to either 23 November or 7 December. Records from the Holiday Inn hotel in Sliema showed that Megrahi had stayed there on the night of 7 December.

The Malta link was confirmed by baggage records from Frankfurt airport, which appeared to show that a suitcase from Air Malta flight KM180 had been forwarded to PA103A. There was no record of any passengers transferring from KM180 to flights PA103A and PA103, and none of the victims were known to own a brown hard-sided Samsonite suitcase. The police inferred from this that the bomb suitcase – known as the primary suitcase – was unaccompanied and that it must have evaded Pan Am's security in Frankfurt.

The explosion occurred within one of the containers that were used to store baggage in the aircraft's holds. The containers were approximately five feet square aluminium or fibreglass-sided cubes, with an extension incorporating a 45-degree angled floor section to accommodate the curved fuselage. The bags were loaded through an open side, which was secured with a curtain when full.

The container in which the explosion occurred was aluminium and had the code number AVE4041. Forensic experts concluded that the centre of the explosion had been around 25 to 30cm above the container's floor and had overhung the angled section by around 5cm. This, the experts claimed, meant that the primary suitcase must have been in one of the following two positions (below and next page, top).

Heathrow ground staff who loaded AVE4041 recalled that, by the time that the feeder flight PA103A arrived from Frankfurt, the bottom of the container was already covered. They said that there were five or six cases standing in a line side-on against the back wall, and two lying flat in front of them, as in the following photograph (next page, bottom).[1]

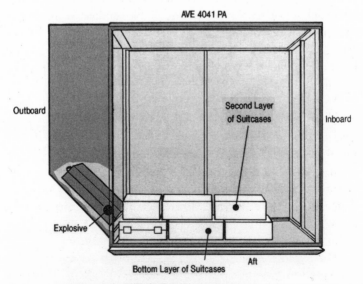

AVE 4041 PA

Outboard

Second Layer
of Suitcases

Inboard

Explosive

Bottom Layer of Suitcases

Aft

FIRST POSTULATED POSITION OF THE IED WITHIN THE CARGO CONTAINER

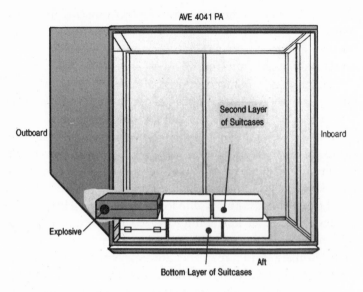

SECOND POSTULATED POSITION OF THE IED WITHIN THE CARGO CONTAINER

Approximate position of luggage before arrival of PA103A.

They had loaded the cases from PA103A on top. As the explosion appeared to have been in the second layer of luggage, it therefore seemed likely that the primary suitcase had arrived on PA103A from Frankfurt.

Megrahi appeared to be a sinister figure. Formerly head of airline security for LAA, he was alleged to be director of the Libyan Centre for Strategic Studies and a partner in a trading company called ABH. Both organizations were said to be fronts for the Libyan intelligence service, the JSO. He was related to some senior JSO figures and regularly travelled on his false Abdusamad passport.

The case against him had three key elements. The first was a fragment of electronic circuit board, which was found embedded in the collar of a blast-damaged, Maltese-made shirt. In 1990 investigators matched the fragment to an electronic timer, known as an MST-13, which was made by a Swiss company called Mebo. The company's co-owner, Edwin Bollier, said the firm had designed and built the timers exclusively for the JSO, and that only 20 were produced. He also revealed that Mebo shared its offices with ABH. He said that in December 1988 ABH's founder, Badri Hassan, had asked him to produce 40 more such timers for the JSO, although he had been unable to fulfill the order.

Megrahi was the common link between Bollier and Malta. There was no doubt that he had visited the island on the night of 20 December using the false passport and had flown back to Tripoli the following morning. He had also been there under his own name on 7 December, which was roughly when Gauci said he sold the clothes. Prosecutors believed that, as a former airline security chief, he would have known how to smuggle a bomb on to an aircraft and that, as LAA's former Malta station chief, Fhimah was well placed to help him.

The second key element arrived on 15 February 1991 when Gauci picked out Megrahi's photograph as resembling the clothes buyer. The third fell into place in July 1991, when

Fhimah's former LAA Malta deputy station chief, Majid Giaka, told the FBI that, at around the time of the disaster, Megrahi had arrived in Malta with a brown Samsonite suitcase, like the one that contained the bomb, and that Fhimah carried it through Maltese customs without it being inspected.

Apart from Giaka, the main evidence against Fhimah was his 1988 diary. A note for 15 December read: 'Take taggs from Air Malta. OK' and 'Abdelbaset arriving from Zurich', while in the back of the diary he had written: 'Take/collect tags from the airport (Abdulbaset/Abdusalam)'. This, the prosecutors believed, showed that Fhimah had obtained an Air Malta baggage tag in order to get the suitcase on to KM180.

* * *

What the prosecutors knew, but failed to reveal, was what their case was full of holes. The weakest link was undoubtedly their most important witness, Tony Gauci. Remarkably, by the time the indictments were issued he had given no fewer than 18 police statements. On many matters his accounts were erratic and contradictory. On two, however, he was entirely consistent – and entirely at odds with the Crown case. The first was the weather at the time of the clothes purchase. He recalled that, as the man was about to leave the shop, he bought an umbrella as it had started to rain. At the crash site the police found the blast-damaged remains of an umbrella, which matched umbrellas sold in the shop. According to the Crown, Megrahi must have bought the clothes on 7 December 1988, as that was the only day he was in Malta. However, Maltese meteorological records obtained by the police indicated that 7 December was dry, whereas there was rain on 23 November, which was the other date on which Paul Gauci was watching football. These facts alone almost destroyed the Crown case.

The second consistent element of Gauci's account was his description of the mystery clothes purchaser. In his first statement, dated 1 September 1989, he said: 'He was about 6 feet or more in height. He had a big chest and a large head. He was well built but he was not fat or with a big stomach. His hair was very black . . . He was clean shaven with no facial hair. He had dark coloured skin . . . I would say that the jacket was too small for him, although it was a 42-inch size, that is British inches.'[2] Megrahi, by contrast, was only 5ft 8in tall, slightly built and light-skinned.

In a further statement, on 13 September 1989, Gauci described the man as being 'about 50 years of age'; however, at the time of the clothes purchase, Megrahi was just 36. A fortnight later Gauci told the police that the shopper had visited his shop the previous day. With the event fresh in his mind, he was able to provide the following clear description: 'This man had the same hairstyle, black hair, no hair on his face, dark skin. He was around 6 foot or just under that in height. He was about 50 years of age. He was broad-built, not fat, and I would say he had a 36in waist.'[3] Clearly, the man's age, height and skin colour ruled out Megrahi.

When Gauci had picked out Megrahi's photograph on 15 February 1991, he initially said none of the 12 photographs were of the man, and only chose Megrahi after being told by Detective Chief Inspector Harry Bell 'to try and allow for any age difference'. Having picked out the photo, he told the police that Megrahi 'would perhaps have to look about 10 years or more older and he would look like the man who bought the clothes. It's been a long time now and I can only say that [Megrahi's photo] resembles the man who bought the clothing, but it is younger.'

Official guidance issued to the Scottish police nine years earlier said photo line-ups should comprise people 'of similar age and appearance', yet most of the other 11 were younger than Megrahi, some of them considerably so. The guidance also advised that: 'The photographs should bear no marks which would enable the witness to identify the suspect's photograph.'[4] DCI Bell had earlier noted that Megrahi's photograph was poor quality, and had therefore asked a Maltese police photographer to re-photograph the others in order to make all twelve of similar quality.[5] Despite these efforts, Megrahi's picture stood out as being paler and grainier than the others. It was also noticeably smaller and had a series of white dots down one side and two white parallel horizontal lines.

Gauci's description of the man as Libyan was far from certain. He said he could distinguish between Libyans and Tunisians, because the latter often reverted to French. However, as most Arabs in Malta were Libyan, many locals described them as 'Libyanos' regardless of their nationality.

Gauci was easily the most important Crown witness, yet Scotland's chief prosecutor, the Lord Advocate Lord Fraser of Carmyllie – the man responsible for the indictments – harboured reservations about his reliability. Almost five years after Megrahi was convicted, and 13 years after leaving office, he told the *Sunday Times*: 'Gauci was not quite the full shilling. I think even his family would say [he] was an apple short of a picnic. He was quite a tricky guy, I don't think he was deliberately lying but if you asked him the same question three times he would just get irritated and refuse to answer . . . You do have to worry, he's a slightly simple chap, are you putting words in his mouth even if you don't intend to?'[6]

The credibility of another key witness, Fhimah's former deputy, Majid Giaka, was also much in doubt. The prosecutors knew that the Libyan was in fact a paid CIA informant. Furthermore, the CIA had made clear to the FBI that, despite having been on the Agency's payroll since before Lockerbie, he had provided no information relating to the bombing.[7] Only two-and-a-half years later did he tell FBI agents that he had witnessed Megrahi and Fhimah with a brown Samsonite suitcase at Luqa airport.[8] By then he had fled Libya in panic, and was desperate for asylum in the United States. He would also have known that he was eligible for a $4 million reward.

Remarkably, neither his FBI and police interviews, nor his subsequent testimony before a US federal grand jury, made mention of his relationship with the CIA. The Agency had dozens of cables in which its agents in Malta reported to their superiors on their meetings with him, yet the head of the FBI's Lockerbie investigation, Richard Marquise, did not request the cables from the CIA.[9] As we shall see in Chapter 4, these documents revealed that, far from being a star witness, Giaka was, at best, wholly unreliable and, at worst, a conman. Even in the absence of the cables, the FBI's alarm bells should have rung when Giaka told them that Colonel Gadafy, the Libyan foreign minister Ibrahim Bishari and the Maltese President Guido de Marco were all freemasons.[10]

There was no hard evidence to support his claim that Megrahi was a senior JSO officer. He acknowledged to the FBI that Megrahi's employer, the Centre for Strategic Studies, was not involved in any type of JSO operations.*[11] Megrahi's only documented involvement with the JSO was a 12-month secondment in 1986 when, as head of airline security for LAA, he oversaw the training of JSO officers who were to be transferred to the airline as part of an organisational reshuffle. Documentary evidence suggested that ABH was a legitimate trading company, which was mainly involved in procuring aircraft spares for LAA, often in breach of US trade sanctions.

Megrahi insisted that his Abdusamad coded passport was issued in order to provide cover for his sanctions-busting, as, unlike his regular passport, it concealed his involvement with the aviation industry. He said that he used it on non-company business for a variety of innocent reasons and pointed out that, as a qualified flight despatcher, he could easily have entered Malta without any official record being made, simply by showing his LAA crew pass.

---

* Megrahi said he was the centre's coordinator, rather than its director, and that his role was essentially administrative.

The Frankfurt airport baggage records provided the next great weak link in the Crown case. They supposedly demonstrated that a suitcase had been transferred from the incoming Air Malta flight KM180 to the Heathrow-bound Pan Am feeder flight PA103A. The key documents were a computer printout from the airport's automated baggage transfer system and a worksheet from a so-called coding station, one of the manned terminals where transfer bags were entered into the system. The system consisted of a huge network of conveyor tracks on which luggage was transferred in trays from the check-in desks and coding stations to the flight departure gates. The printout showed that 111 bags were sent through the system for loading onto the flight, and recorded where each had been logged into the system. The coding station worksheets were supposed to record the originating flight of each batch of luggage dealt with at each station. A detailed analysis by Inspector Jurgen Fuhl of the German federal police, the Bundeskriminalamt (BKA), established that 86 of the bags were checked-in by passengers and the remaining 25 were transfer bags, which were processed at coding stations. By cross-referencing the printout with the check-in and coding station records, Fuhl was apparently able to trace the likely identity of all but two of the bags. One of the two had been processed at coding station 206 at 13.07. The worksheet for station 206 recorded that between 13.04 and 13.10 or 13.16 (it was not clear whether the last digit was 0 or 6) the operators were processing a wagonload of bags from flight KM180.

Unfortunately for the prosecutors, this was far from proof of the Maltese bomb theory. The computer printout demonstrated only that a bag had been sent from station 206 to departure gate 44, from where PA103A later departed.*

---

*The bags were moved around the system in trays. Strictly speaking, the printout showed only that a tray had been sent from coding station 206 to the departure gate. There was no proof that there was a bag in the tray.

There was no evidence that the bag was actually loaded on to PA103A, and less still that it was transferred to PA103 at Heathrow.

The Crown case also relied on the accuracy of the airport workers' time keeping. The computer's time was reset every day by its operators, who were reliant on their watches and the airport's clocks. Even if those devices were accurate, it was known that small fluctuations in the electrical power supply could cause the recorded time to vary by a few minutes. The worksheets were also potentially inaccurate, as they were filled in by hand by staff who were under no particular pressure to record precise timings.[12]

The prosecutors knew that it was possible for airport workers to process bags at unattended coding stations without recording their activities. Just such a scenario was witnessed at station 206 by Detective Inspector Watson McAteer and FBI agent Lawrence Whittaker nine months after Lockerbie, when security should have been tighter than before the bombing. The two officers observed a worker carry a single suitcase to the station and enter it into the baggage system, without making a note or being challenged.[13]

While the Frankfurt records did not prove that a bag transferred from Air Malta flight KM180 to PA103A, far more precise records from Malta's Luqa airport appeared to rule it out. Following a terrorist hijacking there in 1985, in which 58 people died, the Maltese authorities had adopted unusually strict security measures. Military personnel guarded the airport, including the doors of the public check-in area and airside. Baggage-loading procedures were also stringent. All hold luggage had to be physically counted to ensure that the number matched the number checked-in. If it didn't, then all the luggage had to be unloaded and recounted.

The number of bags was recorded independently on two documents, known as the load plan and the ramp progress sheet. The load plan was filled out by the flight's head loader and the ramp progress sheet by the flight dispatcher. The two documents for KM180 both noted the number of bags as 55, which matched the number of legitimate bags that were checked-in and subsequently accounted for by the police.[14]

The dispatcher, Gerald Camilleri, told the police 'I can assure you that 55 was the figure I was given by check-in and 55 was the figure given by the head loader. They reconciled without doubt.'[15] Head loader, Michael Darmanin, was equally certain that the figures reconciled and believed it would have been impossible for anyone to smuggle an extra bag onto the flight.[16]

Neither the Scottish nor the US indictment explained how the two men had got the bomb onto the flight, but a US State Department 'fact sheet' issued to the press at the time of the indictments noted that 'Al-Maqrahi's [sic] flight back to Libya checked-in at the same airport passenger check-in counter as KM180, and the check-in periods for the two flights overlapped.' The implication was that LAA check-in staff had helped him to subvert Air Malta's baggage procedures; however, the police established that Megrahi's flight was checked-in by Air Malta staff.[17]

The forensic evidence that the primary suitcase was in the second layer of luggage within container AVE4041 was also very weak. In 1989 forensic scientists conducted seven explosive tests in the US. In each a replica Toshiba bomb was packed with clothes into a hard-sided suitcase, which was placed within a luggage container like AVE4041 and surrounded with other luggage. Varying amounts of plastic explosive were used, ranging from 360 to 680 grams. According to the final report by Crown forensic scientists Allen Feraday and Dr Thomas Hayes, which was a cornerstone of the indictments, the test results 'confirmed' their assessment of the bomb's location in the second layer of luggage.* However,

---

*The assessment was Feraday's rather than Hayes', as Hayes had little or no involvement in the investigation of the bomb's location.

the test reports revealed that they were far from conclusive. Crucially, the bomb suitcase was positioned in the bottom layer of luggage in only one of the seven tests, moreover the results of that test had been rendered almost useless by a resulting fire.[18] The scientific conclusion was also contradicted by Hayes's examination notes, which observed that the largest piece of the Lockerbie primary suitcase shell appeared to have been in contact with the base of the container when the explosion occurred.[19] This observation was omitted from the final forensic report.

A further major problem for the Crown was the evidence of a Heathrow baggage loader called John Bedford. In early January 1989 he told the police that shortly before going off duty at 5pm on the day of the bombing, he spotted two suitcases lying flat against the bottom of the luggage container AVE4041. One of them, he recalled, was brown, with a hard shell, 'the type "Samsonite" make'.[20] This was potentially highly significant, because he was the only witness from Luqa, Frankfurt and Heathrow airports who recalled seeing such a case.* More importantly, the case could not have been transferred from PA103A from Frankfurt, because that flight did not arrive until well after Bedford had gone off duty, therefore it could not have originated from KM180.

If the prosecutors were right, the Bedford suitcase must have been a legitimate item of passenger luggage. Bedford and his two fellow loaders, Amarjit Sidhu and Tarlochan Sahota, were sure that the entire floor of the container was covered before PA103A arrived. A police reconstruction showed that seven or eight cases would be needed to cover the floor. The only legitimate items in the container prior to PA103A's arrival were so-called interline bags, which meant they had

---

* Bedford's recollection of the suitcase could not have been influenced by media coverage, as at the time he gave his statement the fact that the bomb was contained in a similar suitcase had not been made public.

arrived at Heathrow on other flights. A detailed analysis by the police suggested that only six such bags should have been in the container, so, if the true number was seven or eight, then at least one of them was illegitimate. Furthermore, none of the legitimate bags were brown and hard-sided.

In the absence of credible eyewitness evidence, the Crown case was heavily reliant upon the credibility of the forensic evidence. Most of the key forensic work was done by Hayes and Feraday, who worked at the Royal Armaments Research and Development Establishment (RARDE)'s forensic explosives laboratory. At the start of the Lockerbie investigation, the lab was generally thought to be among the world's best, but by the time the indictments were issued, in 1991, its reputation had plummeted. The reason was the Maguire Seven miscarriage of justice case.

The seven had been convicted in 1975 on terrorist conspiracy charges relating to the Guildford and Woolwich pub bombings the previous year.* Most of them were related to Gerald Conlon, one of the so-called Guildford Four who were wrongly convicted of the Guildford bombing on the basis of false confession evidence. The seven's conviction rested upon the forensic conclusions of a team of RARDE scientists, including Hayes, which suggested that some of them had knowingly handled nitroglycerine.

Following the Guildford Four's successful appeal in 1989 the government ordered an inquiry into the cases headed by former appeal court judge Sir John May. During the hearings the seven's lawyers discovered previously undisclosed evidence from the RARDE scientists' notebooks, which showed their testimony to be, in May's words, 'wholly misleading.' Although much of May's criticism was directed at the forensic explosive

---

* The seven were Anne Maguire, her husband Patrick, their sons Vincent and Patrick, Anne's brother Sean Smyth, her brother-in-law Giuseppe Conlon (father of Gerald Conlon) and family friend Patrick O'Neill.

laboratory's then head, Douglas Higgs, Hayes was also tainted. While May accepted that, at the time of the crucial tests, the scientists' failure to disclose the results 'was honest but mistaken' in his view, 'before long an element of calculation crept into the continuing failure.' He also noted that some of Higgs' and Hayes' evidence to the inquiry was 'wholly at variance with the evidence given at the Maguires' trial and elsewhere.'[21] He concluded that Maguire Seven's conviction was unsafe and the following year it was overturned at appeal.

The year 1992 saw the collapse of another major terrorist conviction in which the laboratory had played a central role. Judith Ward had been jailed in 1974 for planting a bomb on a coach carrying soldiers and their families on the M62 motorway. Twelve people were killed in the attack and many more injured. Higgs had told the trial court that chemical residue tests proved that Ward had handled nitroglycerine, but her lawyers were able to demonstrate to the appeal court, not only that the tests were flawed, but also that, at the time they gave evidence, Higgs' team, which did not include Hayes or Feraday, were aware that a wide range of innocent substances could produce the same test results as nitroglycerine. The appeal court's judgment noted that the team had taken the law into their own hands and had 'knowingly placed a false and distorted scientific picture before the jury.' It concluded, 'Forensic scientists employed by the Government may come to see their function as helping the police. They may lose their objectivity. That is what must have happened in this case.'[22]

In 1993 Feraday was strongly criticised in an appeal court judgment in the case of John Berry, a British businessman who had been convicted on terrorist conspiracy charges in 1982. The case centred on electronic timers, which Berry had supplied to a Syrian arms dealer. Feraday had testified that the devices had been specifically designed and built for terrorist purposes, a claim made nonsense of by four experts at Berry's appeal. In quashing the conviction the Lord Chief Justice Lord

Taylor of Gosforth noted that Feraday's opinions, while 'no doubt honestly held', had been expressed in terms that were 'extremely dogmatic', and described his conclusions as 'uncompromising and incriminating.'[23]

In 1985 Feraday was involved in the remarkably similar case of Hassan Assali, a Hertfordshire electronics company owner, who was also charged with supplying timers to terrorists. Once again, Feraday testified that he couldn't conceive of an innocent purpose to which the devices might be put.[24] In 2005 the Criminal Cases Review Commission referred the case to the appeal court, having considered reports by a number of electronics experts who were critical of Feraday's claims. The commission noted that the Lord Chief Justice's observations about Feraday in the Berry case 'applies equally to the expert evidence he provided in Mr Assali's case.'[25] In July 2005 the conviction was quashed after the Crown indicated that it would not contest the appeal.

The Lockerbie forensic evidence was riddled with oddities and anomalies, many of which concerned the vital circuit-board fragment, which allegedly originated from a Libyan timer. Known by its police reference number PT/35b, it was supposedly found by Hayes in a blast-damaged shirt collar in May 1989. The collar's police label originally described it as 'cloth', but the word was inexplicably changed to 'debris'. Despite knowing that all electronic debris was potentially of utmost significance, Hayes failed to make a sketch of the item in his otherwise thorough examination notes and, unusually, he altered the notes' page number. Also inexplicably, the fragment was not passed to the Scottish police until January 1990.

A further glaring anomaly concerned the blast-damaged brown checked trousers that in September 1989 had led the police to Tony Gauci. The crucial clue was a label of Gauci's supplier, Yorkie Clothing. Police photographs showed the label to be clearly visible on a fragment of the trousers known as PT/28 along with an order number, 1705, which was positioned close to it. However, police records suggest that when Hayes examined the item in March 1989 the label was not visible. A statement by Detective Constable Callum Entwistle, to whom Hayes showed PT/28 on 21 March noted that, apart from the order number: 'there were no other apparent marks of identification visible on [the] piece at this time.' Entwistle and Detective Inspector George Brown then took a sample of the cloth to various textile outlets in order to determine the trousers' origin, an exercise that would have been unnecessary had the Yorkie label been visible.[26]

When questioned about this anomaly by the Scottish Criminal Cases Review Commission in 2005, Entwistle insisted it was impossible that they could have missed the label, then when shown his statement could offer no explanation for the inconsistency.[27] The commission also sought an explanation from Hayes. Having shown him photos of PT/28, a commission investigator asked him: 'Can you envisage a situation whereby the 1705 might have been discovered by you but that the label was not, at the same time at least, discovered by you?' He replied, 'Not really, no.'[28]

Regardless of the quality of the forensic evidence, there were fundamental flaws in the logic of the Crown case against Megrahi and Fhimah. If the two Libyans had been planning to bomb an aircraft, they would surely have lain low on the night before the attack. Instead Fhimah took Megrahi to visit a Maltese man called Vincent Vassallo, with whom Fhimah had recently established a travel agency. As Megrahi and Vassallo had never met before, the event was more likely to stick in Vassallo's mind than if they were already acquainted; furthermore, Fhimah introduced Megrahi using his real name.[29] Megrahi could have stayed at one of the island's Libyan government-owned hotels, or at Fhimah's flat, but instead he booked in to the Holiday Inn, where there was every chance that he would be recognised by the aircrews who often stayed there. He checked-in under the name Abdusamad, which might have made sense if he was the bomber, were it not for the fact that he had stayed there two weeks earlier under his own name.

If Fhimah had abetted Megrahi by obtaining the Air Malta baggage tags necessary to subvert the airline's security measures, he would surely not have recorded his plans in his diary. Neither would he have left the diary in his travel agency's office for over two years.

There was also a problem with the alleged motive for the crime: Colonel Gadafy's desire to avenge the 1986 US air raids on Libya, which were launched from American air bases in the UK. The raids had been made possible by Prime Minister Margaret Thatcher's decision to allow the aircraft to pass through British airspace. In her memoirs, which were published five years after Lockerbie, she wrote, in justification of her decision: '[The air raids] turned out to be a more decisive blow against Libyan-sponsored terrorism than I could ever have imagined . . . the much-vaunted Libyan counterattack did not and could not take place. Gaddafi had not been destroyed but he had been humbled. There was a marked decline in Libyan-sponsored terrorism in succeeding years.'[30]

Dr Jim Swire wrote to Thatcher to ask why she had written this, when the Lockerbie bombing had been attributed to Libya. She replied that she had nothing to add to the text.

Unfortunately, for the next nine years, the official version of the Lockerbie story received little critical scrutiny. No doubt the real killers could not believe their luck.

Getting Away with Murder 2

If Megrahi and Fhimah were not responsible for Lockerbie, then who was? We may never know, but there is, at least, a persuasive alternative case, which has little to do with Libya and everything to do with Iran and a group called the Popular Front for the Liberation of Palestine – General Command (PFLP-GC). In this story Lockerbie was revenge, not for the 1986 US raids on Libya, but for a far more recent American attack.

On 3 July 1988, Iran Air flight 655, from the Iranian port city of Bandar Abbas to Dubai, was accidentally shot down over the Persian Gulf by a US Navy battle cruiser, the USS *Vincennes*. All 290 people on board were killed, most of whom had been travelling to Mecca for the annual Hajj pilgrimage. The US government immediately claimed that the ship's crew believed it to be under attack by Iranian jet fighters, and had issued ten radio warnings to the plane without response. Two weeks later, in a speech to the United Nations, Vice-President George Bush Snr declared: 'One thing is clear, and that is that USS *Vincennes* acted in self-defense . . . [the incident] occurred in the midst of a naval attack initiated by Iranian vessels against a neutral vessel and subsequently against the *Vincennes* when she came to the aid of an innocent ship in distress.'[1]

All these claims turned out to be untrue. None of the ten warnings were likely to have been received by flight 655; indeed, seven were on frequencies that were unavailable to civilian aircraft. It is possible that one message got through, but that was issued by a neighbouring US Navy vessel, the frigate the *Sides*, just 39 seconds before the *Vincennes* fired on the plane. The *Sides*' commander, David Carlson, had long been concerned by the conduct of the *Vincennes* and its commander, William Rogers, which he and other officers considered to be recklessly aggressive. The *Sides'* radar records showed that, rather than descending towards the *Vincennes*, flight 655 was still climbing after take-off. Having interviewed crew members and studied electronic data and video footage, Carlson also established that the Iranian gunboat had not started the skirmish, but had rather retaliated when pursued by the *Vincennes*. Worse still, the *Vincennes* had continued to pursue the boat after it retreated into Iranian territorial waters. It was not until 1992 that the Chair of the Joint Chiefs of Staff at the time of the incident, Admiral William Crowe, admitted that the *Vincennes* had violated the territorial waters.[2]

All these facts could have been established within a short time of the incident, but the US government preferred to portray the mass slaughter of civilians as an act of heroism. The ship's entire crew was awarded the Combat Action Ribbon and in 1990 President George Bush Snr awarded Captain Rogers the Legion of Merit, in recognition of 'exceptionally meritorious conduct in the performance of outstanding service as commanding officer'. The government never apologised for the killings. It would be eight years before it paid compensation to the victims' families and, even then, it refused to accept blame.

Soon after the shootdown the Iranian government made thinly veiled threats of revenge. President Ali Khamenei promised that Iran would use 'all our might . . . wherever and whenever we decide',[3] while the state radio warned that the attack would be avenged 'in blood spattered skies'. The US government took the warning seriously. Two days after the incident the US Air Force's Military Airlift Command warned its civilian contractors, 'We believe Iran will strike back in a tit for tat fashion – mass casualties for mass casualties.' The likely venue for the attack, it said, was Europe.[4]

In order to exact revenge the Iranians called in the PFLP-GC. The Syrian-based group was the ideal candidate: it had developed a good relationship with the Iranian revolutionary guards and their Lebanese proxies, Hezbollah, and, more importantly, it had a track record of bombing aircraft . Its founder, Ahmed Jibril, had broken away from the Popular Front for the Liberation of Palestine in 1968, as he believed that leader George Habash lacked commitment to the armed struggle.

On 21 February 1970 the group planted bombs on two flights bound from Europe to Israel. The first was an Austrian Airlines flight from Frankfurt via Vienna. As the aircraft reached 10,000 feet, a bomb in the baggage hold blew a large hole in the fuselage. Incredibly, no one was killed and the pilot was able to return safely to Frankfurt. The second bomb was planted in the luggage hold of Swissair Flight 330 from Zurich to Tel Aviv. It exploded at 14,000 feet, killing all 47 passengers and crew. Investigations established that both devices had been built into transistor radios and detonated by pressure-sensitive barometric switches designed to activate at altitude.

In August 1972, the group struck again, this time targeting an El Al flight from Rome to Tel Aviv. A barometric bomb disguised in a record-player exploded at 15,000 feet, but the pilot was able to return the plane safely to Rome. The record-player had been given as a present to two unwitting British women by two Arab men who had befriended them in Rome. The police found and arrested the men, who said they had been given the device in Yugoslavia by a young Jordanian PFLP-GC member called Marwan Khreesat. Khreesat, the evidence suggested, was the group's master bomb-maker; yet, despite incriminating evidence from the three attacks, he was left untouched and settled down to life as a TV repairman in his country's capital, Amman.

Sixteen years later Khreesat resurfaced in Germany. On 13 October 1988, the West German federal police, the Bundeskriminalamt (BKA), observed him arriving at an apartment on Isarstrasse in the town of Neuss, near Dusseldorf. Already staying at the flat was a senior PFLP-GC commander called

Hafez Dalkamoni, who was the brother-in-law of the flat's owner, a local grocer called Hashem Abassi. Born in Palestine in 1945, Dalkamoni had been one of the PFLP-GC's founding members. Said to be in charge of the group's European operation, he had visited West Germany regularly during the previous few years.

For the first few months after Dalkamoni's arrival the West German authorities did very little. On 2 February 1988 the Israeli foreign intelligence service, Mossad, reportedly warned the BKA that the PFLP-GC was planning to attack US troop trains in West Germany. On 26 April a bomb exploded on a railway line near the village of Hedemünden as a troop train was passing. It was the second such attack in that area in less than nine months. No one was killed in the bombings and it would be a further six months before Dalkamoni was arrested.

By then, there was powerful intelligence suggesting that a major attack was imminent. Israeli sources later claimed that, following the flight 655 shoot-down, Mossad intercepted messages between the PFLP-GC's Damascus headquarters and the Iranian revolutionary guards' base in Lebanon's Bekaa Valley. Shortly afterwards Jibril reportedly travelled to Tehran and, according to US intelligence sources, further meetings took place between Jibril's representatives and the Iranians, in Tehran and Lebanon. The sources claimed that the US National Security Agency had intercepted a telephone conversation between Jibril and the Iranian Interior Minister, Ali Akbar Mohtashemi,* in which Jibril referred obliquely to a number of potential US targets in Europe.[5]

According to retired CIA Middle East specialist Robert Baer, the CIA had established within days of the flight 655 shoot-down that Dalkamoni and another PFLP-GC member, known as 'Nabil', met members of the Iranian intelligence

---

* Mohtashemi was a well-known hardliner, who had previously been ambassador in Damascus and had also helped encourage the growth of Hezbollah.

service, the Pasadaran. The CIA believed that 'Nabil' was Nabil Makhzumi, also known as Abu 'Abid, a Farsi speaker who was acting as Dalkamoni's assistant. He was said to be the PFLP-GC's main contact with the Pasadaran and to have a Pasadaran case officer called Feridoun Mehdi-Nezhad, who had visited Frankfurt in July 1988.

Baer, who was involved in the early stages of the Lockerbie investigation, said the Iranian instructions were 'crystal clear: Blow up an American airplane – in the air in order to kill as many people as possible.' He claimed that Dalkamoni was one of a small group of Islamic fundamentalists in the PFLP-GC who looked to Iran for inspiration, and that Iranian vetting had established that he was 'a true believer who could be counted on to keep his mouth shut if caught.'[6] Baer would not be drawn on his sources, but insisted they were 'as good as it gets'.[7]

Following the PFLP-GC's contacts with the Iranians, the German foreign intelligence service, the Bundesnachrichdienst (BND), passed on a warning to the BKA that a joint commando of PFLP-GC and Hezbollah might be about to attack American installations in West Germany.[8] On 16 September Dalkamoni travelled to Krusevac, in Yugoslavia, where the PFLP-GC's local commander, Mobdi Goben, had an arms cache stored in a safe house. Five days later they were joined by Khreesat.[9] On 5 October Dalkamoni travelled back to the Isarstrasse apartment in Neuss.[10]

The BKA launched a major surveillance operation, codenamed Herbstlaub, meaning Autumn Leaves, against 16 suspected PFLP-GC members in six cities across West Germany. Apart from Dalkamoni and Khreesat, the most senior suspect was Abdel Fattah Ghadanfar, who rented a flat at 28 Sandweg in Frankfurt. He admitted that he too had been in Yugoslavia in October and had met Dalkamoni and Goben in Belgrade.[11]

On 20 October, Dalkamoni called Khreesat and said he was about to receive 'three black tins with lids', 'gloves' and 'paste' from Ghadanfar, and that he (Dalkamoni) would bring 'at least seven white pointed buttons, four of which would be electric.' Khreesat later made a call to Jordan and told a man called Abed: 'I've made some changes to the medication. It is better and stronger than before.' On 22 October the BKA followed Khreesat and Dalkamoni to Frankfurt, where they visited two electrical shops. Two days later they went shopping in Neuss and bought alarm-clocks, batteries, electrical switches, screws and glue. Later that day Khreesat made another call to Jordan and told his contact that he had begun working the previous day and would be finished in two to three days.

BKA didn't dare wait until Khreesat had finished the job. On 26 October he and Dalkamoni were arrested as they were driving away from the apartment. Fifteen others were arrested in simultaneous raids across West Germany, including Ghadanfar. In the Frankfurt apartment the BKA found a huge weapons cache, including mortars, 30 hand grenades, six automatic rifles, fourteen sticks of dynamite, six kilos of TNT and five kilos of the professional terrorist's explosive of choice, Semtex. There was no such arsenal in the Isarstrasse apartment in Neuss, but there was a very significant find in the boot of Dalkamoni's car. It appeared to be a normal Toshiba radio-cassette player, but when BKA technicians examined it, they discovered that it contained 300 grams of Semtex and a barometric detonation mechanism, which meant it could only have been designed to blow up an aircraft. What was more, in the Isarstrasse apartment, BKA officers found other barometric switches and a detonator. Khreesat, it seemed, had started an aircraft bomb production line. Among the items recovered from the Frankfurt apartment were 14 airline timetables, including ones for Lufthansa, Air France, Iberia and British Airways, and some Lufthansa luggage stickers.[12]

The following month the Yugoslavian police raided the PFLP-GC safe house in Krusevac, seizing, among other things, detonators, fuse wire and seven and a half kilos of Semtex.

Goben got away, fleeing to Syria. On Dalkamoni's orders a Frankfurt-based group member, Martin Kadorah, had also visited Goben in Yugoslavia, arriving by bus on 25 October and remaining there until 28 November.*[13]

Within days of the BKA raids, all but two of the PFLP-GC suspects had been released, including, remarkably, Khreesat. The bomb-maker, it transpired, was a mole for both the pro-Western Jordanian intelligence service and the BND. Only Dalkamoni and Ghadanfar remained in custody. They were eventually charged, but only in relation to the troop train bombing. They were convicted three years later, with Dalkamoni jailed for 15 years and Ghadanfar for 12.

***

Two months after the Autumn Leaves raids, on 21 December 1988, Pan Am 103 was destroyed over Lockerbie. Within a week forensic scientists had determined that the Boeing 747 had been brought down by a bomb in the forward luggage hold. By then the PFLP-GC were already the prime suspects.

In mid-January 1989 the first circumstantial link to the group emerged, when a number of charred electronic circuit board fragments were found trapped within a folded aluminium plate that had been attached to the bomb-damaged luggage container AVE4041. Within two weeks, with the help of Toshiba, RARDE scientist Allen Feraday had established that the fragments originated from a Toshiba RT-8016 radio-cassette player. Although this twin-speaker model was rather different to the single speaker BomBeat RT-F453D found in Dalkamoni's car, the Toshiba connection was startling. Three months later the police discovered among the bomb debris a piece of manual for a Toshiba BomBeat RT-SF16 radio-cassette player. As this was an almost identical model to the

---

* On his return from Yugoslavia, Kadorah was arrested by the BKA and detained until 17 January 1989, when he was released without charge.

RT-8016 originally identified by Feraday, he revised his view and advised the police that the bomb had been contained within the BomBeat SF-16. In a subsequent memo to his senior investigating officer, Detective Chief Inspector Harry Bell wrote: 'the significance of the "Bombeat" name cannot be underestimated in the contexts of the circumstantial evidence.'[14] The name even suggested that the PFLP-GC had played a sick joke.

Khreesat's Toshiba bomb had been powered by four AA-sized batteries, which he had connected with short lengths of wire soldered to their terminals. On 25 December Scottish police officers searching the crash site found an AA battery with a piece of wire soldered to one of its terminals.[15] It was sent to RARDE for analysis, but was apparently ruled out as being part of the explosion without any detailed examination notes being made.[16] When, in 2008, Abdelbaset al-Megrahi's legal team sought access to the item, the Crown Office informed them that Dumfries & Galloway Constabulary had been unable to locate it.[17]

In April 1989 the BKA discovered three more Khreesat-made bombs in the basement of the Neuss grocery store owned by Dalkamoni's brother-in-law, Hashem Abassi. Two were built into radio tuners and the third into a Sanyo monitor. Abassi, who had been unaware that he was storing bombs, said that all three devices had been in the Isarstrasse flat when the BKA raided it six months earlier.[18] This raised the srong possibility that another Khreesat bomb had evaded detection and been smuggled on to PA103.

In November 1989 FBI agents Edward Marshman and William Chornyak interviewed Khreesat at the headquarters of the Jordanian intelligence service in Amman. He confirmed that he had, indeed, made a fifth bomb and that it too had been built into a radio-cassette player. He also said that on 24 October 1988, two days before the Autumn Leaves raids, he noticed that the device had gone missing; however, he denied that it was a twin-speaker model like the Lockerbie bomb, and insisted that he had secretly designed all five bombs not to explode.

When interviewed by Megrahi and Fhimah's solicitors in 2000, Khreesat added vital new details. He said that in 1985 he saw a number of radio-cassette bombs in one of the PFLP-GC's houses in Syria, some of which had two speakers and some of which were Toshibas. He also revealed that Dalkamoni had at least one other radio-cassette bomb in Neuss. He recalled:

> Dalkamoni brought a cassette recorder to me. It had already been taken apart to some extent and he asked me to weld a wire to a particular place in the recorder. It was not obvious to me why he was asking me to do this. This had no electronic purpose at all and I got the impression that my loyalty was being tested to see whether I would ask any questions but right after I did this I went with Dalkamoni to his car and he opened his trunk of the car and in the trunk I saw a cassette recorder. I could only see part of it. There was one end of it where there was a speaker. I also saw wires and Semtex.

Crucially, he added: 'I think that the cassette recorder in his car was a Toshiba two-speaker cassette recorder. The one which he asked me to weld a wire to another part of the device was almost definitely a two-speaker cassette recorder. I could not see the make because it was lying face down, but it definitely had two speakers.'

Khreesat was certain about the purpose of the PFLP-GC operation: 'It was made very clear to us by Ahmed Jibril that he wanted to blow up an aeroplane. This was the whole purpose of us being there and in telephone calls to Dalkamoni Jibril repeated on a number of occasions he wanted a plane blown up. In fact the day before we were arrested in a telephone call to Dalkamoni Jibril absolutely insisted that he wanted a plane blown up. Dalkamoni and I travelled to Frankfurt in order to go to the offices of Pan Am to get information about their flight schedules. We did this. There is absolutely no doubt in my mind that Jibril wanted a Pan Am flight out of Frankfurt blown up.'[19]

Who, though, could have carried out the bombing? Dalkamoni and Ghadanfar were in custody at the time and, although all of the others arrested in the Autumn Leaves raids had been freed, PFLP-GC leader Ahmed Jibril must have feared that they remained under BKA surveillance and, therefore, could not risk involving them in a major attack. However, according to Khreesat, there was another senior operative at the heart of the bomb plot who evaded the BKA. Known as Abu Elias, his true identity remains unknown.

Khreesat told the FBI that, when he and Dalkamoni were in Yugoslavia in September 1988, Dalkamoni had told him that they would be joined by Elias, but Elias never came. He recalled Dalkamoni saying on 22 October that Elias had just arrived in West Germany and that he was an expert in airline security. Khreesat believed that, on the day of their arrest, 26 October, Dalkamoni was taking him to Frankfurt to meet Elias.[20]

The leader of the Yugoslavian cell, Mobdi Goben, also implicated Elias. He went further, claiming that the mystery man had run the operation. During Megrahi's trial it emerged that, prior to his death in 1996, Goben had dictated a long memorandum, which narrated his own involvement in the group's operations, including Lockerbie. Some of the detail tallied with facts uncovered by the BKA about the PFLP-GC's West German cell members, and with information volunteered by Khreesat. Goben also revealed that he had personally brought a bomb from Syria to Yugoslavia, which he said had been made by a man called Awad who lived in a Palestinian refugee camp in Damascus.[21] This supported Khreesat's claim that he was not the group's only bomb-maker.

According to former CIA agent Robert Baer, Elias was the 'big, big centre' of the Lockerbie investigation in its early stages. He confirmed that intelligence had indicated that the Autumn Leaves arrests did not derail the PFLP-GC's bomb plot, and that after the raids some of its members held secret meetings in West and East Germany, Sweden and elsewhere.[22]

The continuing commitment, following the Autumn Leaves raids, of hard-line Palestinians to hit an American target in Europe was underlined in a warning received by the State Department's Office of Diplomatic Security just three weeks before Lockerbie. A departmental digest of the warning, which was circulated on 2 December, stated: 'Team of Palestinians not assoc[iated] with Palestinian Liberation Organisation (PLO) intends to atk [attack] US tgts [targets] in Europe. Time frame is present.' Remarkably, it continued: '[Targets] specified are Pan Am airlines and US mil[itary] bases.' Although the PFLP-GC was not named, the group was opposed to the PLO and had an infrastructure in Europe.

It was the first of two warnings of an attack on Pan Am that was received by the US authorities within a few days. On 5 December the US Embassy in Helsinki received a call from a man who suggested that one of the airline's flights from Frankfurt would be hit in the next fortnight. He named three people, who he said would plant the bomb on an unsuspecting Finnish woman.[23]*

---

* The three named by the caller were an Arab Finnish resident called Yassan Garadat, a Frankfurt resident, whom he called Abdullah, and someone called Mr Soloranta. He claimed that Garadat and Abdullah were members of the Abu Nidal Organisation (ANO), which had a bloody history of anti-Western terrorist attacks in Europe, and which, like the PFLP-GC, was opposed to the PLO. Abdullah, he warned, would give Garadat a bomb, which he would plant on an unidentified Finnish woman. The Finnish police established that
(note continues next page)

The US government claimed that the Helsinki warning had been thoroughly checked out and found to be a hoax; however, on 13 December a memo summarising the warning was posted on the staff notice board of the US embassy in Moscow. It stated that: 'The FAA reports that the reliability of the information cannot be assessed at this point, but the appropriate police authorities have been notified and are pursuing the matter . . . In view of the lack of confirmation of this information, post leaves to the discretion of individual travellers any decisions on altering personal travel plans or changing to another American carrier.'[24] It's not known how many Embassy staff changed their flights as a result of the warning, but a consular official later recalled there being 'a real push in the Embassy community to make sure that everybody was aware that there had been a terrorist threat made, and that people flying Western carriers going through such points as Frankfurt should change their tickets.'[25]

The Scottish police knew that the answer to the question *Who planted the bomb?* might well lie in the answer to *How did they do it?* Within ten days of the bombing it appeared that they had an answer. American and British sources leaked to the press that the bomb had been planted on a young Lebanese American passenger called Khaled Jaafar.[26, 27] The 20-year-old had spent the previous six weeks with Arab acquaintances in

(note continued)
Garadat was unconnected to the ANO, or any terrorist group, and concluded that the caller was a Helsinki-based Palestinian called Samra Mahayoun, who bore him a grudge. Nevertheless, the reference to Mr Soloranta was intriguing, because a well-known ANO commander called Samir Kadar had married a Finnish woman called Soloranta. Kadar was reported to have died in Athens in July 1988 when a car carrying explosives blew up shortly before an attack on a tourist ship, the *City of Poros*, in which nine people were killed and 90 injured. However, some doubted the story, as his body was too badly damaged to identify and it was considered surprising that such a senior figure would be involved at the frontline of a major operation.

Dortmund, which was about an hour's drive away from Neuss, at the opposite end of the Rhein-Ruhr conurbation. Prior to that he had spent a few months with his family in Lebanon's Bekaa valley, which was one of the main strongholds of the PFLP-GC's ally Hezbollah. The valley was also notorious for drug production, and members of the wider Jaafar clan were said to be heavily involved in the trade. Some Scottish police officers searching the crash-site were briefed to look out for heroin, as an unnamed young male Arab passenger was suspected of carrying it.[28] Jaafar was the only such person on the flight. At least two consignments of the drug were found at the crash-site, one by a farmer[29] and the other by a volunteer dog handler (see Chapter 6).[30] Four months after Lockerbie the *Sunday Times* reported that Washington sources had revealed that there were heroin traces within the crash debris and that the bombers may have duped a drug courier into carrying the radio-cassette bomb.[31]

One of Jaafar's fellow passengers on the Frankfurt to Heathrow flight PA103A recalled him being 'very agitated and nervous' when queuing at passport control. She recalled that he did not have any hand luggage,[32] however, his father Nazir Jaafar initially said that he had two items of hand luggage and hadn't checked-in any bags.[33] Pan Am's check-in records recorded that he had, in fact, checked-in two items. Two of his bags were recovered from the crash-site, but it was far from certain that they were the ones he had checked-in. Neither bag bore traces of a check-in label and no corresponding labels were found loose at the crash-site. Both were much smaller than normal check-in bags: one was well within the airline's hand luggage limit and the other was barely over it.[34] Given that his journey home would have taken at least ten hours, it would have been unusual if he had taken no hand luggage. The bags' contents also suggested that they had not been checked-in; for example, there was paperwork relating to his various journeys, and there were no towels and toiletries, which most travellers would take with them when away from home for a long period.[35] If the two bags were hand luggage, it raised the strong possibility that one of his checked-in items had contained the bomb.

In his deathbed memorandum, the PFLP-GC's Mobdi Goben claimed that Abu Elias had planted the bomb on an unsuspecting Jaafar.[36] In 2000 a PFLP-GC associate of Goben's, who claimed to have been in charge of finance for the group's military division, told Megrahi and Fhimah's lawyers that the group had paid substantial sums to a man called Khaled Jaafar. The witness, who went under the name 'Rabbieh', said he could not confirm that it was the same Khaled Jaafar, although someone had told him that it was.[37] There was no evidence to directly link Jaafar to those arrested in the Autumn Leaves raids; however, there were intriguing circumstantial links between a number of them and certain of his Dortmund associates.

There was a viable alternative to the Jaafar dupe theory, which centred on the suitcase seen in luggage container AVE4041 by Heathrow loader John Bedford prior to the arrival of the Frankfurt feeder flight PA103A (see Chapter 1). In the official version of the Lockerbie story, both the Jaafar and Bedford scenarios were put to the sword by the documentary evidence that emerged from Frankfurt airport, which suggested that an unaccompanied suitcase from Air Malta flight KM180 had been transferred on to the Frankfurt to Heathrow flight PA103A.

Even if we ignore the many flaws in that evidence, and accept that the bomb came from Malta, PFLP-GC involvement remains likely, because the group had a strong link to the island through a terrorist called Mohammed Abu Talb. The Swedish-based Egyptian was a member of the Palestinian Popular Struggle Front, which, like the PFLP-GC, was part of the anti-PLO coalition known as the Salvation Front. In June 1985, together with two of his brothers-in-law and another associate, he carried out three bomb attacks in Copenhagen against a synagogue, the offices of the Israeli airline El Al and the US airline Northwest Orient. One person was killed and 22 injured. The same gang was thought to have carried out a similar attack on El Al's Amsterdam office later that year and one on the Stockholm office of Northwest Airlines in April 1986.

One of the brothers-in-law shared an apartment in Talb's adoptive hometown of Uppsala with Ahmed Abassi, the brother of Hafez Dalkamoni's Neuss landlord. Two weeks before the Autumn Leaves raids, on 13 October 1988, the other brother-in-law drove from Sweden to Dalkamoni's Neuss apartment where Dalkamoni and bomb-maker Marwan Khreesat arrived the same day. He stayed overnight and returned to Sweden the following day.[38] A week later, on 22 October, Ahmed Abassi arrived in Neuss and was later observed visiting local electrical shops with Dalkamoni and Khreesat.

Earlier in October Talb had spent two weeks in Cyprus, his first three days on the island coinciding with Dalkamoni's presence there. On 19 October he flew from Cyprus to Malta, where he spent time with two Palestinian brothers.[39]

He returned to Sweden on 26 October, which, by coincidence, was the day of the Autumn Leaves raids in West Germany. On 1 November, based on information received from the BKA, the Swedish Security Police, the Säkerhetspolisen (SAPO), arrested Talb and several of his associates. Although they were all released without charge, on 18 May 1989 he was arrested again in connection with the 1985 and 1986 bombings, together with three of his brothers-in-law and 12 others. When SAPO searched Talb's house they found stored under a bed electrical components, 14 wrist watches, some of which had parts missing, and a barometer, which was missing its barometric mechanism. They also discovered four passports belonging to Talb and two burnt ones, the names of which were obscured.[40]

Whatever the truth of Talb's October visit to Malta, there is no doubt that he returned to Sweden with some Maltese clothes. Although none could be linked to Tony Gauci's Mary's House shop, the police understandably suspected that he was the mystery clothes buyer. The purchase had occurred on or after 18 November 1988, because that was the date upon which brown Yorkie checked trousers found at Lockerbie had been supplied to the shop. There was no evidence that Talb travelled to Malta under his own name after 26 October, but there remained the possibility that he had travelled under a false name and passport.

On 2 October the police showed Tony Gauci a freeze-frame image of Talb from a BBC *Panorama* programme. Although he noted some differences to the customer, he told the police, 'I can state that the photograph I was shown is similar to the man that came in to my shop although I am unable to say that it is definitely the same person.'[41] If the police thought they had got their man, they were to be disappointed, because on 6 December Gauci failed to pick him out from a photo-line-up.[42] Talb was, in fact, no more like the customer described by Gauci than was Megrahi. Gauci had consistently described the man as around 50 years old, about 6 feet tall and well-built, whereas Talb was 36, more slightly built and, thanks to an old battle injury, walked with a limp, which Gauci was likely to have noticed.[43]

If Talb was not the clothes purchaser, it was possible that his role in the bomb plot was to obtain the clothes for the primary suitcase. The Scottish police certainly did not accept his claim that he had brought clothes from Malta as samples for Swedish clothes shop owners. A police report noted that the story 'appears to be a pack of lies'.[44] One of the garments he brought back from Malta was a sweater with the word 'Malta' on the front and SAPO also retrieved from his house two Maltese-made T-shirts, one of which also had a 'Malta' logo on the front.[45]

Apart from the Malta connection, the main evidence that convinced the police to shift focus from the PFLP-GC and Iran to Libya, was the circuit-board fragment, PT/35b. Found in the blast-damaged collar of a Maltese shirt, it appeared to match circuit boards designed by the Swiss firm Mebo for use in its MST-13 timers. When company boss Edwin Bollier told the police that only 20 such timers were made, all of which were supplied to Libya, it seemed clear that the Gadafy regime was involved in the bombing. However, in 1993 Bollier revealed that not all of the timers had been sold to Libya. He said he had given at least two to the East German intelligence service, the Stasi, to which he had been a supplier for around 20 years.[*46] This was potentially significant because the Stasi also supplied Palestinian terrorist groups. East Berlin was a regular destination for a number of PFLP-GC members, including Hafez Dalkamoni, who passed through on his way back to Neuss from Cyprus on 5 October 1988.[47] One of Bollier's Stasi handlers, who went by the cover name Wenzel, admitted to the BKA that, while working for the Stasi, he had built IEDs for use outside East Germany, including a car bomb. He later became secretary to the head of the Stasi's Department 22, which supplied various anti-Western terrorist groups, including the Carlos Weinrich group and the Red Army Faction.[48]

Even if the fragment had originated from a Libyan timer, it did not prove that Libya had carried out the bombing. The

---

* Bollier later claimed that, unlike the MST-13 timer supplied to Libya, which contained green circuit boards made to order by a small Swiss company called Thüring, those supplied to the Stasi timer contained grey-brown coloured prototype boards made by Mebo technician Ulrich Lumpert. If true, this appeared to rule out the Lockerbie fragment as having originated from a Stasi timer. However, Lumpert, who had built the timers, said he had used green Thüring boards in all the timers. Although after the Libyans' trial he changed his story in line with Bollier's, Bollier's Stasi handler, 'Wenzel', said that Bollier had told him the timers contained circuit boards produced for Mebo by a small Swiss company.

Gadafy regime had supplied weapons to numerous terrorist groups, including the IRA, ETA, the Abu Nidal Organisation and, crucially, the PFLP-GC, and it was quite possible that the supplies included MST-13 timers. However, it was a possibility to which neither the Libyans, nor the Scottish and American prosecutors, cared to admit.

Exactly how the PFLP-GC may have executed the bomb plot remains unclear. The most likely scenarios are the duping of Khaled Jaafar and the planting of the bomb in AVE4041 at Heathrow. The former would probably have required the collusion of someone at Frankfurt airport who switched one of his checked-in suitcases with one containing a bomb. It is possible that this person was unaware of the bomb and believed that the case contained drugs. The Heathrow scenario would most likely have involved the suitcase seen by John Bedford before the arrival of PA103A from Frankfurt. It appeared to be placed in the optimum position for the relatively small explosive charge to destroy the aircraft, which suggests either that the terrorists got lucky or that whoever put it there knew exactly what they were doing. Strikingly, the bomb exploded 38 minutes after take off, which was similar to the Khreesat bombs examined by the BKA.* Unlike Luqa, Frankfurt and Heathrow were huge, anonymous complexes with relatively lax security.† If the group had been stupid enough to send the bomb from Malta, then it's likely that Talb was meant to help

* Of the four Khreesat-made bombs recovered by the BKA, one exploded, killing a BKA technician, and another was subsequently destroyed. The remaining two were analysed by BKA expert Rainer Gobel. He established that the radio-cassette device found in Dalkamoni's car would have detonated between 47 and 52 minutes after take off, while the other, which was housed within a Sanyo monitor, would have done so between 37 and 42 minutes after.

† In January 1989 it was established that 779 Heathrow Airports Ltd passes had been reported lost or destroyed. At the time terminal 3 was being redeveloped, which meant there were many construction workers on-site.

organise it, but his arrest on 1 November 1988 probably put paid to his involvement. It seems more likely that his role was to organise the clothing purchase, in order to divert attention from West Germany and Sweden to Malta. The elusive Abu Elias was clearly a far more important player than Talb. Unfortunately, unlike Talb, he evaded justice.

A Nation Condemned 3

Arguably the biggest scandal of the Lockerbie case is the one that is least talked about, at least outside Libya. As a consequence of the flawed charges against Megrahi and Fhimah, and the UK and US governments' subsequent actions, the Libyan people were subjected to seven years of biting sanctions, which contributed to thousands of deaths, drove millions into poverty and caused untold other hardships.

The story is all but ignored, perhaps because it was considered barely newsworthy in the West. The shameful process began less than a fortnight after the indictments were issued against Megrahi and Fhimah, when the UK and US governments issued a joint declaration to the UN Security Council that made four demands of the Libyan government: 1) hand over the two men for trial; 2) disclose all it knew about the bombing, including allowing access to witnesses, documentary evidence and the remaining MST-13 timers; 3) accept responsibility for the actions of its officials; and 4) pay compensation for the bombing.[1] The last two demands were not conditional upon the suspects being found guilty. In effect, then, Libya had been convicted without any of the evidence being tested in court.

By contrast, the Libyan government's actions were in line with existing international law. The basis of that law was the 1971 Convention for the Suppression of Unlawful Acts against the Safety of Civil Aviation, known as the Montreal Convention. Under article 7, if those accused of attacking a civil aircraft were not extradited, then the country in which they were apprehended was, 'without exception whatsoever', obliged to prosecute them. Therefore, as Megrahi and Fhimah were both apprehended in Libya,* and, as the country had no extradition treaties with the UK and the US, the Libyan government had a legal duty to prosecute them.

In keeping with article 6 of the convention, a Libyan judge was appointed to investigate the case. The Libyan government contacted the British and American authorities and requested their cooperation, but they refused, thus breaching article 11 of the convention. In the absence of any evidence to test, the investigation quickly stalled.

Under article 14 of the convention, any dispute between countries that could not be settled through negotiation should, at one of the countries' request, be submitted to arbitration. If, after six months of the request, the parties could not agree on a forum for the arbitration, then any party could refer the case to the International Court of Justice. In January 1992 the Libyan foreign minister, Ibrahim Bishari, wrote to the UK foreign secretary Douglas Hurd and the US Secretary of State to offer arbitration, but his letter was ignored.[2]

The UK and US governments chose to sidestep the convention and use the UN Security Council to force Libya into submission. Article 33 of the UN Charter obliges disputing nations to 'first of all seek a solution by negotiation, inquiry, mediation, conciliation, arbitration, judicial settlement, resort to regional agencies or arrangements, or other peaceful means of their own choice.' Instead the two governments successfully pressured the Security Council to adopt a resolution that condemned the Libyan government for not meeting their joint demands and increased the pressure on it to comply. The resolution – number 731 – was adopted by the Security Council on 21 January 1992.[3] Libya refused to buckle. On 31 March a second British-American sponsored resolution – number 748 – was adopted, which imposed economic and diplomatic

* While Megrahi was in Libya at the time the charges were announced, Fhimah was in Tunisia, but was not apprehended until his return.

sanctions on the country. Most significantly for ordinary Libyans, all international flights were banned* along with the supply and servicing of aircraft and aircraft components.[4] It was the first time that the Security Council had used its coercive powers to compel a country to surrender its citizens for trial abroad.[5] In November 1993 the Security Council adopted a third British-American resolution – number 883 – which tightened the sanctions against the airline industry and banned the supply of oil-refining equipment.[6]†

In early 1992 Libya filed a case with the International Court of Justice alleging that the two governments had acted illegally, and arguing that all parties should be bound by the Montreal convention.[7] In response the two governments claimed that whatever rights Libya might have under the convention were superseded by resolutions 748 and 883. The ICJ was therefore obliged to rule on this matter before it considered the substance of Libya's claim. It would take six years to do so.

In the meantime, the Libyan government continued to pursue a reasonable solution. Most significantly, it offered to hand over the suspects for trial in either a neutral country, or at the ICJ. In early 1994 it accepted in principle a comprehensive proposal by Scottish law professor Robert Black that a trial be held under Scottish law and legal procedures, but in a setting outside Scotland, such as the ICJ. The prosecution would be led by the Lord Advocate and the defence conducted by independent solicitors and counsel. The only significant difference to a standard Scottish trial, apart from the venue, was that an international panel of five judges, presided over and chaired by a Scottish high court judge, would replace the

---

* Excepting flights with a humanitarian purpose.

† The ease with which the UK and UK governments managed to get the resolutions adopted was remarkable, and was a measure of US primacy in the wake of the collapse of the Soviet Union and the US's defeat of Iraq in the 1991 Gulf War.

standard 15-person jury. The proposal was flatly rejected by the UK and US governments, but gained support among the British Lockerbie victims' relatives and the Arab League.

It was not until 1997 that the stalemate began to break. The most obvious catalyst was the Labour Party's general election victory, which resulted in a comprehensive foreign policy review led by foreign secretary Robin Cook, who was quietly sympathetic to the demands of the British Lockerbie relatives.

South African president Nelson Mandela also played a vital role, publicly backing a neutral venue trial and, along with Dr Jim Swire, lobbying Cook at the October 1997 Commonwealth Heads of Government Meeting in Edinburgh.* Significantly, after meeting Swire, Cook said that he did not rule out the suggestion.[8]

In the US the Clinton administration remained, at least in public, hostile to any compromise deal. Although normally the junior partner in the Special Relationship, in this instance the British government proved to be the dominant force, with Cook and Prime Minister Tony Blair eventually persuading Clinton and his secretary of state, Madeleine Albright, to accept in principle a neutral venue trial. Clinton's acquiescence owed much to the fact that his administration was more domestically focused and less doctrinaire in its foreign policy than its immediate predecessors.

The British-American change of stance was driven, as much as anything, by fear of political embarrassment. Thanks to Libya's diplomatic efforts, the sanctions regime had begun to fall apart. In 1997 the annual meeting of Organisation of African Unity's heads of state and government in Zimbabwe raised the possibility that members might unilaterally break the sanctions. The following year they voted to make good the threat by 1 September unless the US and UK governments

---

* Mandela was indebted to the Libyan government for the support it had provided to the African National Congress during its struggle against the Apartheid regime.

agreed to a neutral venue trial. Shortly afterwards the secretary-general of the Arab League warned that its members would follow suit. In November 1997, following a Security Council review of the sanctions,* the Chinese ambassador to the UN, who was presiding over the Council that month, announced to the press that major differences of opinion had been expressed and that China favoured lifting sanctions.[9]

Worse was to follow for the British and Americans. On 27 February 1998, the ICJ finally ruled on whether it had jurisdiction to hear Libya's case under the Montreal convention. The US government had argued that whatever rights Libya had under the convention were superseded by Security Council resolutions 749 and 883, but the Court disagreed.[10] Although the two governments dismissed the ruling as purely technical, it raised the strong possibility that Libya would win the substantive point that they had acted illegally and that the case should be dealt with under the convention.[11]

With the sanctions regime crumbling and international opinion shifting decisively against them, in August 1998, the two governments presented a compromise proposal to the UN Secretary-General. They offered that, as 'an exceptional measure', the trial would be held in a neutral venue, the Netherlands, following normal Scottish law and procedure, except that a panel of three high court judges would replace the jury. Apart from the judges' nationality, the proposal was almost identical to the one suggested by Professor Black, and accepted by Libya, four-and-a-half years earlier.

In April 1999 Megrahi and Fhimah travelled to Kamp Zeist in the Netherlands, where they were taken into custody by the Scottish police. Immediately the UN sanctions were suspended. The event was portrayed in the West as Libya falling into line with the UN's demands. In reality it was a victory for the country's tireless diplomacy and lobbying. Victory, however, had come at a huge cost for the Libyan people.

* The Security Council reviewed the sanctions every 120 days.

Seven years of sanctions had brought the once stable, if sclerotic, economy to its knees. An Arab League estimate suggested that by 1998 the cost to the country had been $23.5 billion. Unemployment rose from 1 per cent in 1992 to 12 per cent in 1996.[12] While the air embargo saw a drop in imports, over the same period food manufacturing fell, by value, from 255.6 to 78.69 million dinars. The government responded with liberalisation measures designed to stimulate private sector imports, but this helped fuel severe inflation. The Economist Intelligence Unit estimated the average inflation rate to be 35 per cent between 1993 and 1997, with a peak of 50 per cent in 1994. Average earnings lagged way behind, leaving most people reliant upon government support. State subsidies of consumer necessities increased nearly seven-fold between 1992 and 1997. Many people had to take second jobs, often as small time traders. Inevitably many became less committed to their main jobs, which in turn undermined public services and the collective values that sustained them.

Despite poor economic management and weak administration, Libya had previously been one of the most egalitarian societies in the Middle East, with the best-paid professionals earning only around five times that of the lowest paid. The growth of a new commercial elite, who had the foreign currency and international contacts necessary to prosper, put paid to this, opening a massive wealth divide. The government attempted price controls, but this stimulated a huge black market, which in turn fuelled corruption and further eroded social cohesion.

While there are few statistics to document the effects of the sanctions of the country's education and health systems, most people experienced a sharp decline in standards. Between 1992 and 1996 no funding was available for university libraries to purchase new books; schools went unrepaired and were unable to spend on new teaching resources; medical equipment broke down and was not replaced, while most medicines became difficult to obtain within the public health system.[13] The Libyan government reported to the UN that the air embargo had led to inordinate delays in the supply of urgently needed vaccines, serums and drugs, and that the increased road traffic had caused a substantial rise in fatal accidents.[14]

Libya lived under the shadow of sanctions for a further four years after 1999. Under the terms of UN resolution 748 the country was obliged to admit responsibility for the bombing and pay compensation to the victims' relatives, regardless of the outcome of Megrahi and Fhimah's trial. In August 2003 the Libyan government wrote to the president of the UN Security Council to formally accept responsibility for the actions of its officials.[15] In December the sanctions were officially lifted. A few months later the government agreed to pay the Lockerbie victims' relatives a total of $2.7 billion. The concessions have been portrayed as an admission of guilt, but in fact they were not. The UN letter was carefully worded to avoid any such admission. In February 2004 the Libyan prime minister, Shukri Ghanem, told the BBC that his government continued to protest its innocence, adding 'We feel that we bought peace. After the sanctions and after the problems we faced because of the sanctions, the loss of money, we thought it was easier for us to buy peace and this is why we agreed on compensation'.[16] Colonel Gadafy's son Saif al-Islam was more blunt, telling the BBC four years later: 'we wrote a letter to the Security Council saying we are responsible for the acts of our employees . . . but it doesn't mean that we did it in fact. I admit that we played with words – we had to. What can you do? Without writing that letter we would not be able to get rid of sanctions.'[17]

At least the Libyans admitted that it was all a big game. So far only one UK or US government insider has publicly presented the story as it really was. Former US State Department lawyer Michael Scharf served as counsel to the department's

counter-terrorism bureau during the Lockerbie investigation
and was later responsible for drafting UN resolutions 731
and 748. Having been convinced by the FBI and CIA of Libya's guilt, he later discovered that their star witness, Libyan
Majid Giaka, was a money-grabbing fantasist. Scharf bitterly
recalled:

> The CIA and the FBI kept the State Department in the
> dark. It worked for them for us to be fully committed to the theory that Libya was responsible. I helped
> the counter-terrorism bureau draft documents that
> described why we thought Libya was responsible,
> but these were not based on seeing a lot of evidence,
> but rather on representations from the CIA and FBI
> and the Department of Justice about what the case
> would prove and did prove. It was largely based on
> this inside guy [Giaka]. It wasn't until the trial that I
> learned this guy was a nut-job and that the CIA had
> absolutely no confidence in him[18] . . . The CIA knew
> all along that this guy was a liar, that this guy was
> just out for money, that they didn't believe half of
> what he said, if any of what he said, and yet they're
> presenting him as the star witness in a case that is of
> such importance? . . . it didn't ruin my career, but it's
> a moment that I'm not proud of.[19]

In an article written shortly after Megrahi was convicted,
he wrote:

> [A]chieving justice was never the main objective. Indeed, the fact that the United States issued a public,
> rather than a sealed, indictment indicates that US authorities never expected that the accused would ever
> actually be brought to trial. Instead, US officials saw
> the indictment itself as a diplomatic tool that would

help them persuade members of the Security Council to impose sanctions on Libya, thereby furthering their goal of isolating a rogue regime.[20]

Whether or not justice was the objective, it was certainly not the outcome of the Lockerbie trial.

A Shameful Verdict 4

On 3 May 2000, Abdelbaset al-Megrahi and Lamin Fhimah went on trial before Lords Sutherland, Coulsfield and Maclean at the specially constructed Scottish Court at Kamp Zeist in the Netherlands. When all the evidence had been heard, eight months later, it was clear to many observers that the Crown case was far from proven; indeed, some considered it to be in ruins.

The key witness against Megrahi was the Maltese shop-keeper Tony Gauci. Megrahi was alleged to have bought the primary suitcase clothing from Gauci's shop on 7 December 1988. The case rested on the shopkeeper's claim that Megrahi resembled the clothes purchaser; however, he acknowledged in evidence that he had described the man as around six feet tall, heavily built, dark-skinned, and around 50 years old. Megrahi, by contrast, was just five feet eight inches tall, light-skinned and, at the time of the incident, was just 36.

On three occasions Gauci had picked out Megrahi as resembling the clothes purchaser, however, he never made a positive identification and there was good reason to doubt all three choices. The first was on 15 February 1991 when he picked Megrahi's photograph from a spread of twelve. He only did so having been told by DCI Harry Bell to ignore any age difference; moreover, he made clear that Megrahi would have to be at least ten years older to look like the man.[1]

The second was on 13 April 1999, a few days after the Libyans had arrived at Kamp Zeist to stand trial, when Gauci picked out Megrahi from an identity parade. He had again been equivocal, telling the police: 'Not exactly the man I saw in the shop ten years ago . . . but the man who look a little bit like exactly is the number five.'[2] The parade took place over seven years after Megrahi and Fhimah were charged with the bombing. During those years Megrahi's image had appeared numerous times in the media. The court heard how, a few months before the ID parade, a neighbour had shown Gauci an article about Lockerbie from a magazine called *Focus*, which featured Megrahi's photograph. Gauci had then shown it to a Maltese police officer, telling him 'That's him'. Small wonder, then, that he was able to pick out Megrahi from the parade.

The final occasion was during Gauci's evidence in chief. Shortly after being shown the magazine photograph, he was asked by Crown counsel to look around the courtroom to see if he could see the man in question. Pointing to the dock, he said, 'He is the man on this side, he resembles him a lot.' When asked which of the two accused he was referring to, he said, 'Not the dark one . . . the one next to him,' meaning Megrahi.[3] Known as dock identification, this procedure is banned in most other Western countries for the obvious reason that an accused person's presence in the dock is highly prejudicial to an objective identification, and the likelihood of a witness looking anywhere other than the dock is minimal. During Gauci's cross-examination the court heard that he had described the clothes purchaser as dark-skinned, which further devalued the dock identification.

Proving the Libyans' guilt required the Crown to prove that the clothes purchase had taken place on 7 December 1988, which was Megrahi's only window of opportunity. Gauci had never claimed to know the date, but told the court that it was about a fortnight before Christmas, at around the time the Christmas decorations were being put up on the street outside.[4] Although this ostensibly favoured 7 December, the Crown could offer no evidence about when the lights were erected and illuminated. Furthermore, the court was told that in 1989 he had said the purchase had occurred before the lights were up.

Gauci had recalled two details that might have helped identify the date. The first was that, on the afternoon in question, his brother was at home watching football on TV. The second was that, as the man left the shop, he bought an umbrella because there was a light rain shower. The police established that the football matches in question were almost certainly on 23 November and 7 December.

Defence witness Major Joseph Mifsud, formerly Malta's chief meteorologist, testified that data collected at Luqa airport on 23 November was consistent with a light rain shower at the time in question. However, equivalent data for the same time on 7 December indicated that it was not raining at the airport. Under cross-examination, Mifsud said that there was, in theory, a 10 per cent chance of some drops of rain falling 5 km away at the shop, but it was just that – a theory. So, not only was there reasonable doubt that 7 December was the date in question, it was almost beyond reasonable doubt that it *wasn't*.

Megrahi's lead counsel, Bill Taylor QC, adduced other evidence that strongly suggested that 7 December was not the purchase date. Mifsud confirmed to him that 8 December was a public holiday in Malta for the Feast of the Immaculate Conception, when, by tradition, all shops were closed. Under cross-examination Gauci acknowledged that the clothes purchase had taken place 'midweek'. When Taylor attempted to define the term, he confirmed that it meant that the shop was open the day before and the day after.[5] Although he was not asked directly whether the shop was open on the day after the purchase, he clearly implied that it was, which again ruled out 7 December.

The defence also severely undermined the Crown's claim that the primary suitcase had originated in Malta. This claim rested on the documents from Frankfurt airport, which supposedly demonstrated that an unaccompanied suitcase from Air Malta flight KM180 had been transferred at Frankfurt airport to PA103A. As well as demonstrating numerous flaws in the evidence, the defence cited the documents from Malta's Luqa airport, and the testimony of Air Malta's former general manager for ground operations, Wilfred Borg, which showed that the number of bags loaded onto the flight tallied with the number that had been legitimately checked-in (see Chapter 1). The Crown could offer no evidence that Megrahi had gone airside at Luqa and neither was there evidence of suspicious activity during the loading of KM180. The defence also called FBI agent Lawrence Whittaker, who, in 1989 had witnessed a Frankfurt airport worker introduce a bag into the airport's automated luggage system, apparently without recording its origin. This demonstrated the ease with which terrorists could subvert baggage procedures. Other witnesses confirmed that all bags transferred onto PA103A from other airlines should have been x-rayed, and that x-ray machine operator, Kurt Maier, had been trained to spot explosives. The court also heard that Heathrow loader John Bedford had recalled seeing a brown, hard-sided, Samsonite-type suitcase in the bottom of the luggage container AVE4041, prior to PA103A's arrival from Frankfurt.

Arguably the Crown's strongest card was the fragment of green circuit board, PT/35b, which was allegedly from the bomb's timer. RARDE forensic expert Allen Feraday testified that it was 'similar in all respects' to circuit boards contained within Mebo MST-13 timers. The company's co-owner Edwin Bollier confirmed that he had supplied 20 such timers to the Libyan intelligence service and that Mebo rented part of its Zurich office to the Libyan company ABH, in which Megrahi was a partner. However, there was no evidence that Megrahi had been involved in procuring the timers. Furthermore, Bollier testified that he had supplied at least two MST-13s to the East German security service, the Stasi, which was known to have armed numerous anti-Western terrorist groups.

Bollier claimed that the Stasi timers contained grey-brown coloured prototype boards made by Mebo technician Ulrich Lumpert, and not the green factory-made boards used in the Libyan timers. However, Lumpert, who had actually built the timers, said that he had used the green boards. Furthermore Bollier's Stasi handler Wenzel recalled Bollier telling him that the timers supplied to the Stasi contained factory-made boards.*

The defence's greatest success came during the cross-examination of LAA's former Malta deputy station chief, the CIA informant Majid Giaka. Supposedly one of the Crown's star witnesses, he left the witness box with his credibility in ruins. Bill Taylor QC and Fhimah's leading counsel, Richard Keen QC, confronted him with extracts from cables by his CIA handlers, which described him as a shirker, whose primary interest was in getting the CIA to pay for sham surgery in order to fake an injury so he could dodge military service. The cables revealed that the handlers were so disappointed with his performance that they had threatened to sack him. It was also clear that he was unable to offer any information of use to the Lockerbie investigation until he had fled Libya and was desperate to get asylum in the US. Only then did he claim to have witnessed Megrahi and Fhimah at Luqa airport shortly before the bombing with a brown Samsonite suitcase.† In one of the trial's lighter moments, Keen asked him six times: 'How did you discover that Colonel Gadafy is a Mason?'[6]

In his final submissions Advocate Depute Alastair Campbell reminded the court that Air Malta's strict baggage procedures would have made it difficult for anyone to get a rogue bag onto flight KM180. He added: 'whatever means was used to introduce the suitcase containing the improvised explosive device, it seems clear that Mr Megrahi would not be able to achieve it alone. He would require assistance from someone in a position to render such assistance at Luqa Airport.' He submitted that Fhimah and Megrahi must therefore have acted together.[7] However, the destruction of Giaka's credibility all but

* Wenzel claimed, unconvincingly, that he had kept the timers as 'demonstration items' and had then destroyed them following the fall of the Berlin Wall in 1989.

† The behaviour of the prosecution and the CIA in relation to the Giaka cables is discussed in detail in the next chapter.

destroyed the case against Fhimah. And, if Fhimah was to be acquitted, then, according to Campbell's reasoning, Megrahi must be too. Sadly, the judges saw things differently.

***

At 11 am on 31 January 2001 presiding judge, Lord Sutherland, flanked by Lords Coulsfield and Maclean, delivered the verdicts in Europe's biggest terrorist murder case. Abdelbaset al-Megrahi was pronounced guilty and Lamin Fhimah not guilty.

Unsurprisingly, the verdicts were major news around the world. Very little coverage was devoted to their lordships' detailed judgment, which was published a few hours later. Many of those who took time to study it were astonished by what they read.

The most obvious flaw with the verdicts was their illogicality. The Crown had contended that Megrahi could not have got the bomb onto flight KM180 on his own and that Fhimah must therefore have helped him, yet Fhimah had been acquitted.* Unfortunately, reason was in short supply throughout the 80-page judgment.

In the penultimate paragraph the judges noted: 'We are aware that in relation to certain aspects of the case there are a number of uncertainties and qualifications. We are also aware that there is a danger that by selecting parts of the evidence which seem to fit together and ignoring parts which might not fit, it is possible to read into a mass of conflicting evidence a pattern or conclusion which is not really justified.' In the view of many observers, however, they did exactly that.

This was apparent in their approach to Tony Gauci. While acknowledging there were 'undoubtedly problems' with his identification evidence, they skirted around the problem in this extraordinary passage:

---

* One of the UN trial observers, Professor Hans Köchler, described the split verdicts as: 'totally incomprehensible'.

Unlike many witnesses who express confidence in their identification when there is little justification for it, he was always careful to express any reservations he had and gave reasons why he thought that there was a resemblance. There are situations where a careful witness who will not commit himself beyond saying that there is a close resemblance can be regarded as more reliable and convincing in his identification than a witness who maintains that his identification is 100% certain. From his general demeanour and his approach to the difficult problem of identification, we formed the view that when he picked out the first accused at the identification parade and in Court, he was doing so not just because it was comparatively easy to do so but because he genuinely felt that he was correct in picking him out as having a close resemblance to the purchaser, and we did regard him as a careful witness who would not commit himself to an absolutely positive identification when a substantial period had elapsed. We accept of course that he never made what could be described as an absolutely positive identification, but having regard to the lapse of time it would have been surprising if he had been able to do so. We have also not overlooked the difficulties in relation to his description of height and age. We are nevertheless satisfied that his identification so far as it went of the first accused as the purchaser was reliable.

Gauci, let us not forget, had consistently described the clothes purchaser as six feet tall, 50-years-old and dark-skinned, whereas Megrahi was 5 feet 8 inches, light-skinned and, at the time of the incident, only 36. The judges were aware that when Gauci first picked out Megrahi's photo more than two years had passed since the incident. Moreover, he said that Megrahi was 'ten years or more' younger than the man. They should have known that the ID parade and dock identification were worthless, and it must also have been obvious to them that, as he had spent his working life in a clothes shop, he was likely to be a good judge of the customer's size.

The judges' approach to the clothing purchase date was even more perverse. In concluding that it was 7 December, they relied on Gauci's testimony that it was about a fortnight before Christmas, even though it was clear that his recollection was only hazy. The meteorological evidence was a much more reliable indicator and was far more consistent with 23 November than 7 December. On the latter date, according to Major Joseph Mifsud, there was theoretically only a 10 per cent chance of some drops of rain falling at Gauci's shop in Sliema. The judges navigated this problem by, in effect, reversing the burden of proof, declaring: 'There is no doubt that the weather on 23 November would be wholly consistent with a light shower between 6.30pm and 7.00pm. The possibility that there was a brief light shower on 7 December is not however ruled out by the evidence of Major Mifsud . . . While Major Mifsud's evidence was clear about the position at Luqa, he did not rule out the possibility of a light shower at Sliema.'

The judgment brushed aside the evidence concerning the public holiday on 8 December, noting: 'We are unimpressed by the suggestion that because Thursday 8 December was a public holiday, Mr Gauci should have been able to fix the date by reference to that. Even if there was some validity in that suggestion, it loses any value when it was never put to him for his comments.'

The judges' willingness to award the Crown the benefit of the doubt was also evident in their treatment of the evidence from Luqa, Frankfurt and Heathrow airports. The only evidence that the bomb had originated from Luqa was the blast-damaged Maltese clothes and the Frankfurt airport documents. The defence had exposed numerous weaknesses in the Frankfurt documents and the clothes, in themselves, proved nothing. Furthermore, flight KM180's check-in and loading records appeared to rule out the possibility of a Luqa originating bomb. While acknowledging that this was 'a major difficulty for the Crown case', the judges preferred the equivocal Frankfurt documents to the far more precise Luqa ones.

They also downplayed the evidence of Heathrow loader John Bedford. They accepted that he was 'a clear and impressive witness'; that the suitcase he saw 'could fit the forensic description of the primary suitcase' and that any rearrangement of the baggage during loading may have resulted in the case ending up in the second layer of luggage, which was where the Crown experts claimed that the explosion had taken place. However, having made these concessions, they added: 'if there was such a rearrangement, the suitcase described by Mr Bedford might have been placed at some more remote corner of the container, and while the forensic evidence dealt with all the items recovered which showed direct explosive damage, twenty-five in total, there were many other items of baggage found which were not dealt with in detail in the evidence in the case.' Proof of Megrahi's guilt required proof that the highly suspicious Bedford suitcase had not contained the bomb, but the judges had relieved the Crown of the responsibility of providing such proof.

The one substantial element of the defence case accepted by the judges was that the Libyan CIA informant Majid Giaka was neither credible nor reliable. However, they made an exception for his claim that Megrahi was a senior intelligence officer. On this basis they concluded, without any corroboration, that Megrahi would have been 'aware at least in general terms of the nature of security precautions at airports from or to which LAA operated.' In the absence of any supporting evidence, there was no justification for selecting elements of Giaka's account that suited their conclusions. But, of course, neither was there any justification for finding Megrahi guilty.

Burying the Evidence 5

A fair trial requires the prosecutors to disclose all evidence that could be helpful to the defence case. In the trial of Megrahi and Fhimah the Crown spectacularly failed in that duty.

The failure first became apparent during an extraordinary episode concerning the Libyan CIA informant Majid Giaka. Prior to the trial the Crown disclosed 25 heavily redacted CIA cables in which his case officers reported on their meetings with Giaka. According to the CIA, there were only 25.[1]

The defence lawyers tried to establish who was responsible for the redactions and what information had been blanked out. In January 2000 Procurator Fiscal Norman McFadyen wrote to confirm that they had been done by the CIA in consultation with lawyers from the US Department of Justice, in order to remove material that was 'irrelevant or potentially damaging to US national security'.[2] The CIA then handed over new copies of the cables in which the redactions were described using general terms such as 'administrative marking', 'operational details' and 'electronic addressing'.

Three months into the trial, on 21 August 2000, during a meeting with defence counsel, Advocate Depute Alastair Campbell QC revealed that McFadyen and Advocate Depute Alan Turnbull QC had seen the unedited cables during a secret meeting at the US Embassy in The Hague on 1 June. Turnbull confirmed the story and said they had done so in order to establish that the Crown had met its disclosure obligations.

Next day Megrahi's counsel Bill Taylor QC told the judges that without access to the complete cables the defendants would be denied a fair trial, adding: 'I emphatically do not accept that what lies behind the blanked-out sections is of no interest to a cross-examiner . . . Further, I challenge the right of the Crown to determine for the Defence what is or is not of relevance to the Defence case.'[3]

Unusually, the Lord Advocate, Colin Boyd QC, responded to the submissions in person. He assured the court that, having seen largely unredacted cables: 'The learned Advocate Depute reached the conclusion that there was nothing within the cables which bore on the Defence case, either by undermining the Crown case or by advancing a positive case which was being made or may be made, having regard to the special defence.'

Lord MacLean asked Boyd if there was any reason why the complete cables should not be disclosed to the defence. He replied: 'Well, my Lord, that is not a matter for me. I do not have control over these documents. They are in the control of the United States, and they are not here. So, I do not have authority to allow access to documents which are not documents which are under my control, or indeed in my jurisdiction.' He then restated categorically: 'there is nothing within these documents which relate to Lockerbie or the bombing of Pan Am 103 which could in any way impinge on the credibility of Mr Majid on these matters.'[4] The judges, nevertheless, invited Boyd to use his best endeavours to have the full cables disclosed.

The reason the Lord Advocate had no control over the documents was that, at the CIA's insistence, McFadyen had signed a non-disclosure agreement, which read: 'I understand that the US Government is providing me access to US national security information solely for the purpose of determining whether it contains any information which is exculpatory to the defendants in the case of the Lord Advocate v Abdelbaset Ali Mohmed Al Megrahi and Al Amin Khalifa Fhimah. Furthermore, I agree not to use this US national security information for lead purposes in furtherance of the Crown's case without the consent of the proper US [Government] official.'[5] In other words, the Crown had secretly ceded to the CIA the right to determine what evidence should be disclosed in a Scottish court.

On 25 August the Crown handed over less redacted versions of the cables, which revealed much new information. It was apparent from the unredacted sections that there had been other meetings between Giaka and the CIA, which were not covered in the 25 cables. Fhimah's senior counsel, Richard Keen QC, told the Court it was 'abundantly clear' that the previously redacted information was highly relevant to the defence, adding: 'I frankly find it inconceivable that it could have been thought otherwise . . . Some of the material which is now disclosed goes to the very heart of material aspects of this case, not just to issues of credibility and reliability, but beyond.'[6] In other words, he believed that the Lord Advocate had seriously, if unwittingly, misled the Court.

The judges asked the Crown to try to obtain further information from the CIA. Following a three-week adjournment, the Crown handed over 36 more cables.[7] Again, the newly disclosed information was highly relevant to the defence case. It revealed, among other things, that Giaka's CIA handlers had asked him specifically about Lockerbie and that he knew nothing, leading them to conclude that the bombing 'may be a non-subject with his colleagues'. Some of the cables indicated the CIA's increasing impatience with his 'demanding nature'. One revealed that he had lied to his handlers about returning to Libya to seek a job, and that they had deduced that he was 'at best . . . a cooperative contact'.[8]

In view of the CIA's concealment of evidence, Taylor requested that it be urged to hand over all the information it held about Lockerbie. He submitted: 'It is perfectly obvious, in our submission, that the Lord Advocate is not master in his own house. It's obvious that he can only disclose to the Defence material of which he is in possession. And it's equally plain that those who have been determining relevancy outside the law of Scotland have made fatal errors of judgement in important areas of direct relevance to this trial, and to its fairness.'[9]

The judges denied a defence petition for letters of request to be sent the US authorities seeking all documents relevant to Giaka. So, thirteen years on, we still do not know whether the CIA concealed other important information.

Nevertheless, armed with both the less redacted and the new cables, Taylor and Keen were able to destroy Giaka's credibility and with it the case against Fhimah. Had the judges accepted the Lord Advocate's assurance, Fhimah might well have been convicted. The basis of that assurance, it seemed, was a memo by McFadyen about his and Turnbull's inspection of the largely unredacted cables on 1 June. The key passage read: 'We were able to satisfy ourselves that there was nothing omitted [from the cables] which could assist the defence in itself. There were some references to matters which in isolation might be thought to assist the defence – eg details of payments or of efforts by Majid to secure sham surgery – but since evidence was being provided as to the total of payments made and of the request for sham surgery, the particular material did not appear to be disclosable. We were satisfied that the material which had been redacted was not relevant to the case or helpful to the defence.'[10]

It was true that evidence had been disclosed of the total payments to Giaka and of a request for sham surgery so he could resign from the intelligence service, the JSO (a.k.a. the ESO). The payments were detailed in two separate CIA documents – not cables – while sham surgery was referred to in one of the disclosed cables. However, the redacted sections, which McFadyen and Turnbull felt were not helpful to the defence, contained numerous references, not only to his desire for sham surgery, but also to his repeated and successful pleas to the CIA to pay for it. One of the cables described him as 'something of a hypochondriac', while another noted his claim to be a distant relative of Libya's former leader King Idris. A further one revealed that he wanted the CIA to set him up in a car rental business in Malta and that his handlers believed that much of the $30,000 that he had saved towards the venture had been acquired from illegal commissions and possibly low-level smuggling.

Crucially, there were also references to meetings with the CIA, for which no cables had been disclosed. Most tellingly, the redactions concealed the agency's increasing dissatisfaction with Giaka. One noted that his information about the ESO's structure and administration 'may be somewhat skewed by his prolonged absence and lack of seniority'. Another revealed that he would be told: 'that he will only continue his $1,000 per month salary payment through the remainder of 1989. If [he] is not able to demonstrate sustained and defined access to information of intelligence value by January 1990, [the CIA] will cease all salary and financial support until such access can be proven again.' A later section of the same cable noted: 'it is clear that [Giaka] will never be the penetration of the ESO that we had anticipated . . . [He] has never been a true staff member of the ESO and as he stated at this meeting, he was coopted with working with the ESO and he now wants nothing to do with them or their activities . . . We will want to ensure that [he] understands what is expected of him and what he can expect from us in return. [CIA] officer will therefore advise [him] at 4 Sept meeting that he is on 'trial' status until 1 January 1990.'[11]

How on earth could McFadyen and Turnbull consider that such information was 'not relevant to the case or helpful to the defence'? There is no suggestion that they deliberately concealed evidence that they knew would help the defence, or that the Lord Advocate deliberately misled the court. However, motive is not the issue: what really matters is the quality of the Crown's judgement. None of the participants were held to account for their role in the affair; indeed, their careers prospered. Turnbull and Boyd are both now senior judges, while McFadyen was promoted to Crown Agent and Chief Executive of the Crown Office and was later appointed a sheriff.

In the years since the trial, it has become clear that the Giaka cables scandal was the tip of the iceberg. Numerous other items of highly significant evidence have since come to light, which, had they been disclosed to the defence, would very likely have resulted in Megrahi's acquittal.

In September 2001, the *Daily Mirror* revealed that at 00.30 on the day of the bombing, a break-in was reported at the Heathrow terminal three. Someone had broken through a locked door that led from the check-in area to the baggage build-up area, where PA103's checked-in luggage was stored prior to loading. The container AVE4041, in which the explosion later occurred, had been left in the build-up area by loader John Bedford at around 17.00, and it remained there, unattended, for around 45 minutes.

The *Daily Mirror*'s source was Heathrow security officer, Raymond Manly, who described the break-in as 'the most serious security breach that I came across in 17 years at Heathrow.' Having given a statement to the police, he was amazed when the incident was not discussed at Megrahi and Fhimah's trial.[12] It was not until 2012 that the police would explain what had happened to the statement. In a letter to Dr Jim Swire the Chief Constable of Dumfries & Galloway Constabulary, Patrick Shearer, explained:

> Mr Manly's statement was passed to the police incident room at Lockerbie and was registered on the HOLMES* system on 2 February 1989. This statement and those from other witnesses identified at Heathrow were considered by enquiry officers at the time in the context of a range of emerging strands of evidence. In 1991 the police report outlining the evidence against Mr Megrahi and Mr Fhima was submitted to the Crown Office. This report did not contain a reference

---

* HOLMES is the Home Office Large Major Enquiry System, a computer system used for major police investigations.

to the insecurity at Heathrow and made no mention of Mr Manly's statement. The surrender of Mr Megrahi and Mr Fhimah for trial in the Netherlands prompted a massive preparation exercise during the course of which over 14,000 witness statements were provided to Crown Office in 1999. Mr Manly's statement was included in the material supplied to Crown though again the police made no reference to it.

So, the police withheld the statement from the Crown Office, prior to the Lord Advocate announcing charges against Megrahi and Fhimah in 1991, and the Crown Office subsequently withheld it from the defence team.

At Megrahi's first appeal, in 2002, the defence argued that the break-in evidence rendered the guilty verdict unsafe. The judges disagreed. It nevertheless remains the only recorded evidence of suspicious activity on the day of the bombing at any of the three airports on which the police investigation was focused.

Only after the Scottish Criminal Cases Review Commission announced its findings in June 2007 did the full extent of the Crown's disclosure failures began to emerge. The commission referred Megrahi's case back to the appeal court on six grounds, a remarkably high number. More remarkably still, four of those grounds involved non-disclosure.

The first one concerned the date of the clothes purchase at Tony Gauci's shop. When interviewed by the defence prior to the trial, Gauci said he thought the date was 29 November. This was startling, because the Crown claimed it was 7 December, Megrahi's only window of opportunity. If Gauci had repeated the claim at trial, Megrahi should have been acquitted, but, when asked during the interview why that date had stuck in his mind, he replied: 'all I can say is that is what I think.'[13] When the SCCRC investigators checked Gauci's Crown precognition statements they discovered that he recalled the date because he had had a row with his girlfriend. The SCCRC concluded that, by withholding the statement, the Crown had deprived Megrahi of a potentially important line of defence.[14]

The second of the non-disclosure grounds concerned Gauci's exposure to media articles about the case. The court had heard that, in late 1998 or early 1999, a neighbour had shown him an article in *Focus* magazine featuring Megrahi's photo. Gauci had handed it over to Maltese police officer superintendent Godfrey Scicluna, and had pointed to the photo saying, 'That's him.' The court was left with the impression that Gauci had possessed the article for only a short time. The SCCRC discovered a statement by another Maltese officer, sergeant Mario Busuttil, which showed that the handover was not until 9 April, which meant that the photo would have been fresh in his mind when he picked out Megrahi at the identity parade at Kamp Zeist just four days later.[15]

The SCCRC's investigators also discovered a confidential police report, dated 20 March 1999, which noted the problems caused to Gauci by the increasing media coverage of the case. It revealed that in early 1999 Gauci had been given two detailed articles on the case which had appeared in the Maltese-language newspaper *It Torca*.[16] Gauci told the SCCRC that people came into his shop 'every day' with newspaper articles, and also said he had seen Megrahi's photos on TV news items.[17] His brother Paul Gauci revealed that he collected articles about the case, which he kept at home. He said 'there was practically an article every week' as well as programmes on the BBC, and said that he relayed their contents to Tony.[18]

The SCCRC concluded that Gauci's exposure to photos of Megrahi created a substantial risk that Megrahi would be instantly recognisable to him, even if he had no genuine memory of the purchaser. It added that both the Busuttil statement and the police report were likely to have been 'of real importance in undermining the Crown case' and therefore should have been disclosed.[19, 20]

The SCCRC's third non-disclosure ground concerned the discussion of reward payments to the Gauci brothers. The investigators discovered an extract from DCI Harry Bell's diary, dated 29 September 1989, which recorded a conversation that Bell had that day with FBI agent Chris Murray. According to the note '[Murray] had the authority to arrange unlimited money for Tony Gauci and relocation is available. Murray states that he could arrange $10,000 immediately.' It added, 'Murray was advised that no facilities are to be used without Bell's knowledge and consultation with the Maltese authorities.'[21]* The SCCRC was unable to establish whether the FBI had put the offer to Tony, but other documents confirmed that he had first expressed an interest in rewards prior to picking out Megrahi's photograph on 15 February 1991. One of the documents confirmed that he was 'aware of the US reward monies which have been reported in the press.'[22] Another confidential police report, dated 10 June 1999, described him as being 'somewhat frustrated that he will not be compensated in any financial way for his contribution to the case.' It added that the police had taken great care never to offer him inducements to testify and described him as a 'humble man who leads a very simple life which is firmly built on a strong sense of honesty and decency.' However, it gave a very different view of his brother Paul, stating: 'It is apparent from speaking to him for any length of time that he has a clear desire to gain financial benefit from the position he and his brother are in relative to the case. As a consequence he exaggerates his own importance as a witness and clearly inflates the fears that he and his brother have. He is anxious to establish what advantage he can gain from the Scottish police.' Significantly, it added: 'Although demanding, Paul

---

* When asked by the SCCRC whether FBI agent Chris Murray had ever met with Gauci to discuss a reward, DCI Bell replied, 'I cannot say that he did not do so'. He also revealed that FBI agent John Hosinski had met with Gauci alone on 2 October 1989, but said he doubted that money had been discussed and was insistent that the $10,000 offer had never been put to Gauci.

Gauci remains an asset to the case but will continue to explore any means he can to identify where financial advantage can be gained. However, if this area is explored in court with this witness however (sic) he will also strongly refute that he has been advantaged.'[23]

In another police report, written in January 2001, shortly before the end of the trial, an unidentified officer wrote: 'The issue of financial remuneration has not previously been discussed in detail with the witnesses and no promises exist.' However, earlier in the report the officer had noted that: 'It is considered that the witnesses may harbour some expectation of their situation being recognised', which implied that the brothers had delayed the resolution of these issues in the expectation that they would receive a reward.

The report emphasised that 'whilst proceedings were still 'live' they displayed a clear understanding that such matters could not be explored,' but continued: 'It is considered that the implementation of the foregoing recommendations will ensure that when the inevitable reflections and media examinations take place in future years the witnesses who are the subject of this report will maintain their current position and not seek to make adverse comment regarding any perceived lack of recognition of their position. Nor is it anticipated they would ever seek to highlight any remuneration received.'[24] This seemed to imply that, if the brothers were paid, they could be relied upon not to embarrass the police or Crown.

Another memo, written after the trial, reiterated that rewards had not been discussed with the brothers until the trial had ended, and added: 'The motivation of both witnesses has never at any stage been financial, as can be seen from their refusal of money from the media. They have received no financial gain from the Scottish police; as a result, their integrity as witnesses remains intact. This has been the priority from the outset.' It said of Tony, 'The very fact that the witness was not motivated by financial gain and as a result his integrity as a crucial witness was maintained, reinforces the need to ensure that at this stage his contribution and more importantly the manner of his contribution is recognised.' However, it said of Paul: 'it should never be overlooked that his major contribution has been maintaining the resolve of his brother. Although younger, Paul has taken on the role of his father (died 7 years ago) with regard to family affairs. His influence over Anthony has been considerable (It is considered critical that the contribution of Paul is recognised in order to preserve their relationship and prevent any difficulties arising in the future).'[25] 'Paul's 'considerable' influence over his brother was highly significant given what the 10 June 1999 memo described as his 'clear desire to gain financial benefit.' Furthermore, the police's refusal to discuss rewards was irrelevant, because it was clear from the earlier documents that the brothers were interested in being paid.

The SCCRC also unearthed two important letters by Senior Investigating Officer Detective Chief Superintendent Tom McCulloch. The first, written a week after the trial verdict, to the US Embassy in The Hague, nominated Gauci for a US government reward.[26] The second was sent shortly after Megrahi's unsuccessful first appeal in 2002 to the Deputy Chief of the US Department of Justice's Terrorism & Violent Crime Section. In it McCulloch wrote:

> At the meeting on 9 April, I proposed that US 2 million dollars should be paid to Anthony Gauci and US 1 million dollars to his brother Paul. These figures were based on my understanding that US 2 million dollars was the maximum payable to a single individual by the Rewards Programme. However, following further informal discussions I was encouraged to learn that those responsible for making the final decision retain a large degree of flexibility to increase this figure. Given the exceptional circumstances of this case . . . I would invite those charged with approving the reward to

ensure that the payments made to Anthony and Paul Gauci properly reflect not only the importance of their evidence, but also their integrity and courage.

McCulloch reported that, at the Americans' suggestion, he had discussed the reward application with Crown Office. He explained: 'The prosecution in Scotland cannot become involved in such an application. It would therefore be improper for the Crown Office to offer a view on the application, although they fully recognise the importance of the evidence of Tony and Paul Gauci to the case.' In other words the Crown Office was prevented by its own rules from seeking a reward for Gauci, but saw no problem with the police doing so.[27] The SCCRC established that Tony and Paul were paid under the US Government's Rewards for Justice programme[28] and respective awards of at least \$2 million and \$1 million have never been denied.*

As the SCCRC noted, Gauci's trial evidence was, in some respects, more helpful to the Crown than the police statements that he had given years earlier. In those statements he had described the clothes purchaser as around 50 years old and six foot or more in height, but he told the Court, 'I think he was below six feet. I'm not an expert on these things, I can't say'[29] and 'I don't have experience on height and age.'[30] The commission also noted that the *Focus* magazine article,

---

* When interviewed by the SCCRC, Tony Gauci denied ever asking for money and disputed the contents of DCI Bell's memo of 21 February 1991. He said that his brother only raised the subject after the trial. Paul said that the police had offered a reward, but confirmed that he had insisted on being paid after Megrahi's first appeal was over. He said he was not present at the meetings referred to in Bell's memo, but Bell told the SCCRC that the meetings would have involved Paul, and that Paul had pushed for a reward to compensate his family for the difficulties that the case had caused. He insisted that that rewards were not discussed with Tony when he picked out Megrahi's photo on 15 February 1991.

which he had for three and a half months, highlighted the fact Megrahi was much younger and smaller than the man he had described.[31] When interviewed by the commission, Gauci confirmed that someone had read him that passage of the article, so he must have been aware of the problems that his evidence might cause the Crown.[32] While there is no suggestion that he deliberately twisted his testimony to suit the prosecution case, there was a great danger that he might have done so unconsciously.

The SCCRC's fourth non-disclosure ground concerned two secret intelligence documents, which had been supplied to the British government by an unnamed foreign government. The SCCRC was prohibited from copying the documents and revealing their contents. The Crown Office confirmed that it had them pre-trial and had concluded that it was not legally obliged to disclose them. The SCCRC took a different view, concluding that the non-disclosure may have resulted in a miscarriage of justice.[33]*

The commission discovered other undisclosed evidence that would have been helpful to Megrahi's defence. This included a report, written by DCI Harry Bell in early October 1989, concerning Gauci's claim, made in a statement on 26 September, that the clothes purchaser may have visited the shop the previous day. In it Bell revealed: 'He [Tony] now states that

* The content of the two documents remains a mystery. The SCCRC's statement of reasons provided only two clues. The first was an extract of a letter from the Crown dated 27 April 2007, which stated, 'it has never been the Crown's position in this case that the MST-13 timers were not supplied by the Libyan intelligence services to any other party or that only the Libyan intelligence services were in possession of the timers.' The second came in paragraph 25.6 of the statement of reasons, which said that, in concluding that a miscarriage of justice may have occurred as a result of the documents' non-disclosure, the commission has taken into account paragraphs 49, 73 and 74 of the Trial Court's judgment.' Since paragraphs 49, 73 and 74 all referred to MST-13 timers and the PFLP-GC, it seemed very likely that the documents also did.

he can only be 50% sure that it was the same "Man" in the shop on Monday 25 September 89. The question now is with an apparent ability to recall in detail events of November and possibly December 1988 coupled with his recollection of the "Shooting trip" several years ago Tony can only be 50% sure of a week-old sighting. DCI Bell pointed out that Tony was still under pressure from his father and brother Paul not to give information.'[34] If Gauci was only 50 per cent certain of a sighting just a week earlier, then it severely diminished the reliability of his later partial identifications of Megrahi, the first of which was well over two years after the incident.[35]

Another previously secret document revealed that earlier in September, against Bell's wishes, Maltese officer Godfrey Scicluna had shown Gauci a photo line-up because he thought that Gauci's description of the clothes buyer matched someone he knew. The document noted that, although Gauci had failed to pick anyone out: '[He] said that the suspect had a hairstyle identical to No 2 (afro-style) and the facial features of No 20.'[36] The reference to the Afro hair was potentially very important, because, together with Gauci's original description of the suspect as 'dark', it strongly suggested that the man was black. The Crown Office claimed to have no record of the fax, but when SCCRC investigators checked a corresponding file at MI5 they found a note suggesting that Crown officials had viewed it in March 2000.[37]

The SCCRC was apparently unaware of the significance of some of the documents that it had unearthed, which were contained in the report's appendices. One such was a classified police memo, dated 3 April 1990, by DC Callum Entwistle, which described a visit by French police officers who were investigating the 1989 bombing of French airline UTA's flight 772 over Niger.* It revealed that the senior investigating

---

* UTA flight 772 was blown up on 19 September 1989, killing 170 people. As with Lockerbie, the initial evidence pointed to Iranian-backed militants, but eventually Libya was blamed.

officer, Detective Chief Superintendent Stuart Henderson, told the French delegation that the crucial circuit-board fragment, PT/35b, had been tested for residues and found to be negative, owing to 'the total consummation of the explosive material.'[38] This directly contradicted the trial evidence of Dr Thomas Hayes, who testified that he did not test the fragment for explosive residues because it was clear that it was bomb-damaged.[39] There is no suggestion that Hayes deliberately misled the trial court and it is possible that residue tests were conducted on the fragment without his knowledge. Nevertheless, had the defence lawyers been aware of the document, it would have allowed a more vigorous cross-examination of Hayes.

The appendices also included two Crown precognition statements of Hayes' RARDE colleague Allen Feraday. In the first he revealed that he had been unable to exclude the possibility that one of the debris items that he had examined, PI/1588, was part of a barometric trigger, a fact he had omitted from the Crown forensic report.[40] As both he and the Crown knew, the PFLP-GC bombs found in West Germany were barometric. As the Crown also knew, the statement was relevant to the special defence of incrimination lodged by the defence, which named some of the PFLP-GC suspects.

The second statement concerned the forensic criteria that Hayes had developed in order to distinguish primary suitcase clothing from that in the surrounding luggage.* Feraday commented: 'Tom Hayes established the criteria and I did not feel comfortable using them . . . The more precise the criteria, the greater the number of items which will fall on the borderline . . . It is so difficult to be precise about such classifications.

* Hayes concluded that clothes that contained bomb fragments, such as black plastic from the casing of the Toshiba radio-cassette player, but no luggage fragments, were considered most likely to have been in the primary suitcase, while those containing no fragments, or ones including luggage fragments, were more likely to have been in the other luggage.

I would not have adopted such strict criteria for the clothing.'[41] Hayes's clothing categorisation system was central to the Crown's case, because it provided the forensic basis for the claim that the clothes from Tony Gauci's shop were in the primary suitcase. Here was his closest colleague casting doubt on the system, yet the Crown considered it unnecessary to share these doubts with the defence.

Some very important Crown documents remained undiscovered by the SCCRC. One such was a statement by Detective Inspector Watson McAteer concerning the incident that he and FBI agent Lawrence Whittaker had witnessed at Frankfurt airport in September 1989, in which an airport worker had apparently coded a single item of baggage into the luggage system without recording the transaction (see Chapter 1). Whittaker was one of just three defence witnesses called by Megrahi's lawyers. When asked by defence counsel David Burns QC if he had mentioned the incident to anyone, he replied: 'I discussed it with Detective McAteer, and at a later point we mentioned it to the German officers with whom we had liaison.' During cross-examination he was asked by Advocate Depute Alan Turnbull QC, 'Do I take it that you would not be close enough to see whether this particular worker made an entry in a notebook?' He replied, 'It would be very likely that that could have been missed, yes.'[42] This left the court with the impression that the airport worker may well have recorded his action.

McAteer's statement gave a substantially different account. It noted, unequivocally, that the worker had completed the transaction 'with no entry being made on the work sheet', and that he and Whittaker had questioned an airport supervisor, who conceded that such practices were not unusual.[43] This crucial document was not disclosed to Megrahi's lawyers until 2009.

Probably the most important undisclosed evidence concerned the fragment of circuit board PT/35b, which was allegedly from the bomb's timer. Easily the strongest element of the

Crown's case, it was the golden thread that linked Megrahi and the bomb to the clothes from Tony Gauci's shop.

The case relied on the claim that PT/35b originated from one of the 20 MST-13 timers that were supplied to Libya by Mebo. The circuit boards in these timers were designed by Mebo specifically for use in the timers, and made to order by the small Swiss company, Thüring. So, if the Crown case was true, PT35b must have originated from one of the Thüring circuit boards.

Mebo had ordered far more circuit boards from Thüring than it had used in the Libyan timers. Fortunately, it had kept the spare boards, and in 1990 Bollier handed them to the police, along with two control sample timers, which also contained original Thüring boards. They were examined at RARDE by forensic scientist Allen Feraday. In his subsequent report, written with Dr Thomas Hayes, he stated that it had been 'conclusively established [that PT/35b's] materials and tracking pattern are similar in all respects' to the MST-13 circuit boards. He repeated the claim when giving evidence at the trial. 'Similar in all respects' was a term that he and Hayes used repeatedly in the report when describing items that were clearly of common origin.

The forensic report was completed in December 1991. A few months later, in spring 1992, Feraday's conclusion appeared to be supported by a series of scientific tests conducted by an array of academic and circuit board industry experts. The same experts had done similar tests on PT/35b in early 1990, when the police were trying to determine its origin. The 1992 tests were conducted on one of the Thüring boards supplied by Mebo, in order to establish whether there was a material match with PT/35b. The results suggested that there was, however, there was one, apparently minor, difference, which was noted in the reports of two scientists, Dr Rosemary Wilkinson, a metallurgist at Strathclyde University, and Dr David Johnson, an analytical chemist at the Centre for Surface and Materials Analysis, a commercial consultancy attached to the University of Manchester Institute of Science and Technology. Both scientists analysed the boards' copper circuitry and the thin layer of tin plating, also known as tinning, which is used to coat the copper in order to help manufacturers to solder on components. The tests on PT/35b indicated that the plating was pure tin, whereas that on the control sample, which had the police reference number DP/347a, gave quite high readings for lead as well as tin. Both scientists speculated that the difference might have resulted from PT/35b's proximity to the explosion. Wilkinson pointed out that lead has a low boiling point and that the heat might have caused any lead in PT/35b's plating to evaporate. She advised that her hypothesis be tested by experiment, but there is no evidence that the police commissioned such experiments.[44]

The scientists' reports were all disclosed to the defence pretrial; however, the defence made no issue of the tin-plating difference and Feraday's crucial assertion that PT/35b was 'similar in all respects' to the Thüring boards remained unchallenged.

In 2009 that assertion was proved to be untrue. The difference, it transpired, was not an insignificant anomaly, but was rather because the tin on PT/35b was fundamentally different from that on DP/347a. Megrahi's appeal team learned that in circuit-board manufacturing 'tin' is a generic term that can mean either pure tin,* or a tin-lead alloy. Some boards are plated with pure tin and others with tin-lead alloy, and the manufacturing processes required to produce each type of plating are often different. It was clear that PT/35b was plated with pure tin and the control sample, DP/347a, with a tin-lead alloy. Crucially, Thüring's production manager, Urs Bonfadelli, who had made the boards used in the Libyan timers, told the

---

* I have used the term 'pure tin' for simplicity's sake, but, strictly, it is a misnomer as that type of plating generally contains very small traces of other metals. 'Lead-free' is a more accurate term.

appeal team that the firm only ever used a tin-lead alloy, which was normal in the industry at the time.[45]

It was clear that the only way that PT/35b could have originated from one of the Thüring-made boards, and therefore from one of the 20 Libyan timers, was if – as Wilkinson and Johnson had speculated – the heat of the explosion had changed its plating from a tin-lead alloy to pure tin. Megrahi's solicitor, Tony Kelly, instructed metallurgist Dr Jess Cawley to test the hypothesis. He subjected replica fragments, plated with a tin-lead alloy, to far greater heat energy than PT/35b could have been exposed to during the momentary flash of a Semtex explosion. He then analysed them with a scanning electron microscope to see if the lead had disappeared. It hadn't. In other words, if the plating of a Thüring circuit board had been exposed to an explosion, it would not have changed from tin-lead to pure tin.[46] Kelly also instructed circuit board manufacturing expert Dr Chris McArdle, who concluded that PT/35b's plating had been produced by a different manufacturing processes to DP/347a's.[47]

Taken together, all this meant that the PT/35b could not have originated from a Thüring circuit board, which in turn meant it could not have come from one of the 20 Libyan timers. The strongest element of the case against Megrahi and Libya had therefore been destroyed.

It initially seemed that neither Feraday, nor the police, had been aware of the very significant difference between PT/35b and the Thüring circuit boards, but, shortly before Megrahi's return to Libya, the Crown disclosed three documents that suggested otherwise.

The first two contained the results of previously secret metallurgy tests that had been conducted on PT/35b and the control sample DP/347a at RARDE. Each document contained a handwritten note by Feraday, dated 1 August 1991. The note for PT/35b stated: 'Plating on tracks is of pure tin'. The one for DP/347a said: 'Tinning on the thin tracks is of [approx]

70/30 Sn/Pb.' Sn and Pb are respectively the chemical symbols for tin and lead. Unlike the scientists consulted by the police, Dr Rosemary Wilkinson and Dr David Johnson, Feraday was an electronics expert who should have recognised the significance of the difference that he had noted.

After the note on DP/347a's plating, he had conjectured: 'However this may be dipped or roller tinned on top of either the Cu [copper] tracks? Or the Cu tracks with a layer of pure tin?' In other words DP/347's tracks may have been plated with pure tin, which was, in turn, plated with tin-lead. As well as being scientifically unfounded, this presupposed a method of double-plating that was not used in any type of standard circuit board manufacture. Was he, perhaps, trying to account for the difference between the two items by suggesting that in PT/35b's case an outer tin-lead plating had been lost to the explosion, leaving a layer of pure tin? If the fragment had been double-plated the two layers would have melted into each other during manufacture, meaning that it was impossible for a layer of pure tin to remain distinct beneath the outer layer of tin/lead alloy.

The documents' true significance was in demonstrating that Feraday was aware of a very significant dissimilarity between PT/35b and the Thüring control sample. Why, then, did he state, both in his report and his court evidence, that the items were 'similar in all respects'?*

It is not known whether Feraday notified the police and Crown Office of the dissimilarity prior to the Lord Advocate issuing the indictments against Megrahi and Fhimah in November 1991. If he did, then the Crown Office should have

---

* In his report and trial evidence Feraday was careful to note another, arguably less significant, difference between PT/35b and some of the control sample Thüring circuit boards, which was that the PT/35b, in common with the first batch of boards ordered from Thüring, had solder mask on one side, whereas boards in the second batch were solder-masked on both sides. (Solder mask is a resin used to protect the circuitry from hot solder.)

known that the forensic basis of the indictments was fatally flawed. What is beyond doubt is that the police were aware of the evidence by the time Megrahi and Fhimah's trial began in May 2000, because each of the documents bore a Dumfries and Galloway Constabulary stamp dated 8 November 1999. At that time, the police were interviewing witnesses and collecting evidence on behalf of the prosecution team. The documents should therefore have been passed on to the prosecutors. If they were, then their significance should have been apparent and they should have been disclosed to the defence. If a decision was taken not to disclose the documents, it is likely that it was justified on the grounds that the defence would have been alerted to the dissimilarity between PT/35b and DP/347a by the statements and reports of Dr Wilkinson and Dr Johnson. However, none of those statements and reports hinted at the significance of the dissimilarity, because neither scientist was an electronics expert. Moreover, unlike Feraday, neither of them had made a crucial forensic claim in a disclosed document that was contradicted by their own findings. If the prosecutors had the two documents, they should have known that disclosing them to the defence would have enabled a tough cross-examination of Feraday.

The only official comment upon the new forensic evidence came from RARDE's successor organisation, the Defence Science and Technology Laboratory (DSTL) in answer to a question posed by the producers of a TV documentary. As I explain in Appendix 1, the response was unfounded nonsense.

The third important document disclosed to Megrahi's lawyers shortly before his return to Libya was a lengthy police memo dated 16 March 1990, written by DI William Williamson for the Senior Investigating Officer Detective Chief Superintendent Stuart Henderson. It summarised what the police investigation had, by then, discovered about the fragment and described the various expert analyses that had been conducted, including the metallurgy tests. The crucial passage read: 'Without exception it is the view of all experts involved in the PCB [printed circuit board] industry who have assisted with this enquiry that the tin application on the tracks of the circuit was by far the most interesting feature. The fact that pure tin rather than a tin-lead mixture has been used is very unusual.'

Three months after Williamson wrote the memo, the police's Lockerbie inquiry team learned that PT/35b appeared to match circuit boards in the MST-13 timers and three months after that, in September 1990, they learnt that MST-13s were made by Mebo. The company's co-owner, Edwin Bollier, told the police that the circuit boards used in the timers had been made to order by Thüring and provided the paperwork to prove it. As the police were aware that PT/35b's pure tin coating was unusual, they should have asked Thüring's production manager, Urs Bonfadelli, what type of plating was used on the Mebo boards. Had they done so, they would have learned that their carefully constructed case against Megrahi and Fhimah was built on sand.

By early March 1992 both Dr Wilkinson and Dr Johnson had reported that the control sample Thüring board DP/347a had a tin-lead alloy coating. Given what the police knew about PT/35b, this should have been enough to alert them to the fact that the fragment did not originate from a Libyan timer, even if they were unaware of the test results recorded by Feraday six months earlier.

There is no suggestion that Williamson and Henderson acted improperly, but had the Williamson memo been disclosed before Megrahi and Fhimah stood trial, the defence lawyers would have been alerted to the 'very unusual' comment and would have been able to pursue the issue with Bonfadelli and so destroy the central element of the Crown's forensic case.

So, why were the three crucial documents not disclosed? In February 2013 I asked this question of the Crown Office under the Freedom of Information (Scotland) Act and also asked who was responsible for the decisions. Under the Act, it should have responded within 20 working days, unless there were public interest considerations, in which case it should have informed me within that 20-day limit. It failed to respond until 18 June, when I received a refusal letter from John Logue, the senior procurator fiscal for the East of Scotland, who was formerly a member of the Lockerbie prosecution team. He explained: 'While we recognise that there is some public interest in release [of the information] because it relates to the Lockerbie bombing which remains a significant event in Scotland and to Mr Megrahi's conviction, this is outweighed by the public interest in withholding information because of the ongoing criminal investigation into the involvement of others with Mr Megrahi in the bombing and the possibility of further legal proceedings in relation to Mr Megrahi's conviction.'* Revealing why the documents were not disclosed, and who made the decisions, could not possibly jeopardise 'the ongoing criminal investigation into the involvement of others'. It might well, of course, jeopardise the reputations of the Crown Office and its officers.

Although I was entitled to request the Crown Office to conduct an internal review of the refusal, the likelihood that one of Logue's colleagues would overturn his decision was minimal. Section 47(1) of the act allows a general right to appeal internal review decisions to the Scottish Information Commissioner, but, handily for the Crown Office, section 48 exempts it from that provision. In other words, it is the final arbiter of whether or not its information should be made public. No other Scottish public authority enjoys this cocoon of secrecy.

---

* The 'possibility of further legal proceedings in relation to Mr Megrahi's conviction' appeared to be a reference to a police investigation of complaints of alleged criminal misconduct made by the committee of the Justice for Megrahi campaign group – see chapter 7.

A Bigger Picture 6

Let us be clear, there was no grand conspiracy by the intelligence services, senior politicians, police officers, prosecutors and judges to subvert the Lockerbie investigation and frame Megrahi and Libya. Conspiracies, of course, do sometimes happen, but seldom ones involving so many diverse parties.

There is, however, no doubt that important evidence was suppressed, that US intelligence agents interfered with the crash site and that some of the evidence against Megrahi was highly dubious. It can also be reasonably argued that the case against Libya was concocted in order to serve the agenda of the government of US president George H. W. Bush, who came to power less than a month after the bombing.

In all these things the Scottish authorities were, very likely, no more than unwitting accomplices. There are allegations – not made by this book and so far unproven – that certain of their representatives acted illegally. If they did, it was almost certainly in order to secure the conviction of people they sincerely believed to be guilty, and not because they were party to a wider plot to protect the real culprits and convict innocents.

To understand why Bush's people might have laid a false trail to Libya, it is important to understand two things about the presidency of Ronald Reagan, in which Bush was vice-president. The first is that it was deeply mired in illegal arms deals with Iran; the second is that it was obsessed with toppling the Libyan leader, Colonel Muammar Gadafy.

The Iranian arms deals arose from another of the Reagan administration's obsessions, the fate of US hostages held in the Middle East. In November 1979, a year after Iran's Islamic revolution, a group of radical students stormed the US embassy in Tehran and took 52 American staff members hostage. The

14-month crisis proved disastrous for Democratic President Jimmy Carter, and undoubtedly lost him the 1980 presidential election to Reagan.

Having ridden to power on a hostage crisis, those closest to Reagan and Bush were hypersensitive to the issue's political toxicity, especially their election campaign manager, William Casey, whom Reagan had appointed CIA director. During the early and mid-1980s a number of American citizens were taken hostage in Lebanon by Shia militants with close ties to Iran's Revolutionary Guards. Most alarmingly for the Reagan administration, they included the CIA's Beirut station chief, William Buckley. In November 1986 it emerged that Casey and a motley array of National Security Council (NSC) staff members and former intelligence agents had organised a secret supply of weapons to Iran – then officially deemed to be a terrorist state – in return for the release of the hostages. Some of the profits from the arms sales were diverted to the illegal funding of the so-called Contras, the anti-government forces who were waging a terrorist war against the left-wing government of Nicaragua. The scandal, which became known as Iran-Contra, rapidly escalated and for many months threatened to topple both Reagan and Bush.

The White House remained desperate to contain the fallout throughout Bush's presidency, which ended in January 1993. Its efforts were largely successful. Crucially, it was broadly accepted that operation was run by over-zealous mavericks in the NSC, most famously Lt Col Oliver North, and that Reagan and Bush were asleep on watch, rather than centrally involved. However, evidence that emerged through various official inquiries, in particular that conducted by independent counsel Lawrence Walsh, tells a very different story. Some of this evidence was omitted from the inquiry reports, which were limited in their scope and, in some cases, clear whitewashes. It was pieced together over the last 25 years by a few dedicated investigators, most notably the American journalist

Robert Parry, who was among the first to break the Iran-Contra story.

The evidence suggests that the genesis of Iran-Contra was not the Lebanese hostage issue of the mid-1980s, but rather the presidential election campaign of 1980, when Reagan and Bush were preparing to fight Carter. A few months before the election, Casey learnt through various contacts – some Iranian – that Carter was secretly trying to negotiate the release of the Tehran hostages. Knowing that, if successful, Carter would very likely win the election, Casey deployed a team of former CIA officers to monitor the initiative. In the event, it failed and the hostages were held until Reagan's inauguration day in January 1981.

In the early 1990s a number of witnesses came forward independently with claims that Reagan's campaign team stymied Carter's deal with a deal of their own, which involved supplying weapons to Iran in return for delaying the hostages' release until after the election. At the heart of the deal, it was alleged, were Casey and Bush. The witnesses claimed that Casey met Iranian representatives in Madrid at the end of July 1980, and that Bush and others, including the later CIA director and defence secretary Robert Gates, had similar meetings in Paris on the weekend of 18 and 19 October. Leading the negotiations for the Iranians, they claimed, was Mehdi Karroubi, who later became chair of the Iranian Parliament and is now a leading opposition figure. Among the witnesses was Iran's then president Abolhassan Bani-Sadr.

This alleged scandal, which became known as October Surprise, was potentially far more damaging to Bush than Iran-Contra: selling weapons to a terrorist state was bad enough, but negotiating the extended captivity of US citizens for crude political ends was far worse. According to Parry, probably the main reason that Bush wanted to fend off the Iran-Contra scandal was that he knew it could lead to the unravelling of October Surprise.

Predictably, the October Surprise allegations were rubbished by Bush's people and by friendly journalists, who trumpeted supposedly cast-iron alibi evidence for Bush and Casey. A congressional investigation in 1992-3 also cleared the president. Over the years, however, Parry and others have accumulated documentary and witness evidence that corroborates the original allegations and proves some of Bush and Casey's alibis to be false. Parry's investigation also demonstrates the extraordinary lengths to which Bush went to thwart the October Surprise and Iran-Contra investigations.

Against this background, it is easy to see why the first Bush administration did not want the Lockerbie bombing to be blamed on Iran. But, even if Iran-Contra and October Surprise are discounted, the hostage issue was still a huge preoccupation for the White House. Both it and the UK government knew very well that, if they had blamed Iran and the PFLP-GC for Lockerbie, it would have endangered the American and British hostages who were being held in Lebanon. In this context it can surely be no coincidence that within days of Megrahi and Fhimah being indicted – at which point the two governments stressed that Lockerbie was a purely Libyan operation – the last American and British hostages were released from Lebanon.

The Reagan administration's other obsession, Libya, was nurtured by Casey and other rabid neoconservatives who had the president's ear. Like the post 9/11 neocons,* they believed that a muscular foreign policy was vital to the US's moral renewal, and they found a perfect vehicle for it in the 'War on Terror'. Whereas the current neocons allege a global jihadist conspiracy, Reagan's people claimed there was a global terrorist network controlled by the Soviet Union. Their holy scripture was *The Terror Network*, a best-selling book by journalist Claire Sterling. The claims came as news to CIA and State

---

* A number of prominent neoconservatives from the Reagan era, such as Dick Cheney, Donald Rumsfeld and Richard Perle, went on to serve the second President Bush.

Department analysts, who warned that there was little or no evidential support. The agency's chief Soviet Affairs analyst, Melvin Goodman, warned Casey that the book was mainly recycled disinformation, but Casey wouldn't have it. 'When we looked through the book we found very clear episodes where CIA black propaganda, clandestine information that was designed under a covert action plan to be planted in European newspapers were picked up and put in this book . . . a lot of it was made up,' Goodman later recalled. 'We told them that point blank and we even had the operations people to tell Bill Casey this [but] Casey had made up his mind. He knew that the Soviets were involved in terrorism, so there was nothing we could tell him to disabuse him. Lies became reality.'[1]

At the heart of the terror network, Sterling and the neocons proclaimed, was the 'Daddy Warbucks of terrorism', Libya's Colonel Gadafy,[2] who rapidly became public enemy number one. As State Department analyst Lillian Harris wryly observed, 'Gadafy presented this marvellous target because you could fight the Soviets, you could fight terrorism, and you could fight the "evil Arabs".'[3] Just as there was no evidence of a global terror network, there was no evidence that Libya was a Soviet puppet state.

There was no doubt that Libya supported numerous terrorist organisations, including some of the most violent in the Middle East. So too did Syria and Iran, but, unlike those countries, Libya was geographically and politically isolated and, crucially, had no leverage over the US. It also had a loudmouthed, eccentric leader, who perfectly fitted the role of cartoon villain.

As soon as Reagan entered the White House, his government began hyping the Libyan threat. At the same time Casey launched a huge covert CIA campaign against Gadafy[4] and issued a directive to all CIA station chiefs to spread disinformation about Libya.[5] Before long the government was claiming that Gadafy was plotting a huge terrorist campaign in the US.

The plot never materialised, almost certainly because it never existed. The hysteria nevertheless barely subsided for the next five years. During that time the NSC drew up plans for military and covert action designed to topple Gadafy. Many of the staff involved, including Oliver North, were also involved in Iran-Contra. One such was Vincent Cannistraro, a CIA officer who was seconded to the NSC and from 1984 headed its Libya task force. Having later returned to the CIA as chief of operations and analysis of its counterterrorism centre[6] he headed what he termed 'the intelligence side' of the Lockerbie investigation, which involved 'collect[ing] intelligence that would help the law enforcement side find the kind of evidence they would need to bring indictments in a court of law.'[7]

In 1985 and 1986 a series of spectacular terrorist attacks in Europe appeared to give the government the excuse it needed to attack Libya.* In each case the government declared that there was irrefutable evidence of Libyan involvement, but the authorities who investigated the attacks were far more circumspect. The last such attack, on 5 April 1986, was the bombing of a West Berlin nightclub called 'La Belle', which was popular with US servicemen. Two people died and many more were injured.

Within hours the White House declared that Libya was behind the attack. The claim was based on two intercepted cables allegedly sent from the Libyan Embassy in East Berlin to Tripoli. The first reportedly said: 'We have something planned that will make you happy.' The second, sent around the time of the bombing, was translated as: 'An event occurred. You will be pleased with the result.'

The White House refused to hand over the cables for independent scrutiny. Such intelligence traffic was usually analysed by a section of the National Security Agency (NSA)

---

* Among these were the November 1985 Air Egypt hijacking, which resulted in 58 deaths, and the Rome and Vienna airport massacres of December 1985, in which 19 were killed.

known as G-6, but, according to a lengthy investigation for the *New York Times* by journalist Seymour Hersh, the La Belle intercepts went straight to the White House. A NSA official told Hersh: 'The G-6 section branch and division chiefs didn't know why it was taken from them. They were bureaucratically cut out and so they screamed and yelled.' Another said: 'There is no doubt that if you send raw data to the White House, that constitutes misuse because there's nobody there who's capable of interpreting it . . . You screw it up every time when you do it – and especially when the raw traffic is translated into English from a language such as Arabic, that's not commonly known.'*

On 15 April, as a direct response to the La Belle bombing – and in a thinly disguised attempt to kill Gadafy – the US launched air strikes on Tripoli and Benghazi. Scores of people

---

* In 2001 four people connected to the Libyan embassy in East Berlin were convicted of the bombing: embassy official Abdulghasem Eter; Palestinian Yassir Chraidi, whom the embassy employed as a driver; another employee, Lebanese-born German Ali Chanaa; and Chanaa's wife Verana. The key evidence against Eter was contained in the archives of the former East German security service, the Stasi. Three years earlier a TV documentary by German channel ZDF revealed that Chraidi was on the verge of being released owing to lack of evidence when the police and BND made a deal with Eter, which would grant him immunity in return for incriminating Chraidi. The programme confirmed that Eter was involved in the bombing, but also that he was a long-time CIA informant. (In the event he remained a defendant as his cooperation proved to be limited.) ZDF established that another group of terrorists was involved in the attack, but were largely left alone by the German authorities. In the months preceding the bombing their movements were monitored by the Stasi and the Russian intelligence service, the KGB, both of which concluded that the group were working for Western intelligence services. A declassified KGB document indicated that the group's leader, 'Mahmoud' Abu Jaber, was a CIA *agent provocateur* who had been used to concoct a case against Libya. His close colleague, Mohamed Amairi, admitted that he had been working for the Israeli intelligence service, Mossad.

were killed and laser-guided bombs almost destroyed the tent and house in which Gadafy usually stayed.

A few months after the raids, in August 1986, the White House National Security Adviser, John Poindexter, advocated a systematic disinformation programme against Libya, which would involve 'a series of closely coordinated events involving covert, diplomatic, military and public actions.' He proposed a combination of 'real and illusionary events – through a disinformation program – with the basic goal of making Gadafy think that there is a high degree of internal opposition to him within Libya, that his key trusted aides are disloyal, that the U.S. is about to move against him militarily.' The proposals were adopted in a National Security Decision Directive signed by President Reagan, which made clear that the aim of the campaign was to 'bring about a change of leadership in Libya'.[8]

The Lockerbie bombing occurred two years later. There is no doubt that that British and American governments and various western intelligence services interfered with the investigation. Some of this interference occurred at the crash-site immediately after the bombing. The US government denied that any of their officials reached the scene until after 23.00;[9] however, a team of mountain rescue volunteers who arrived in Lockerbie within two hours of the crash found American officials already there. When one of the volunteers reported to the police station he discovered a number of Americans studying maps in a ground floor room. They made clear that he wasn't welcome and told him to leave.[10]

The next day a military helicopter crew was asked to fly two Americans, whom they were told were intelligence agents, to particular parts of the crash site. On arriving at each, the men went off on their own, apparently in search of something. At the second stop they returned with sacks, but did not disclose their contents. Later the same day the crew flew the pair to Glasgow airport, as they were returning to the US.[11]

Nine days later, on 31 December, a Lothian and Borders police officer arrived unannounced on the doorstep of the Labour MP Tam Dalyell to vent his concern that Americans were apparently conducting their own searches of the crash-site without police supervision.[12]

At least two volunteer searchers found themselves circled by an unmarked helicopter in which was seated a marksman with a rifle, while others were prevented from entering certain areas of the crash site. One of these was a field just north of the B7068 a few miles east of Lockerbie, in which a large object was covered by a red or orange tarpaulin. The object was later taken away on a low-loader and its identity remains unknown.[13] There was another temporary no-go area on Carruthers Farm a few miles south-east of Lockerbie, where farmer Innes Graham was ordered by two plain-clothed Americans to stay away from a particular hill.[14]

Another farmer found a number of large packages of white powder within a suitcase that was on his land. When he reported it to a police officer, the officers implied that the powder was drugs and contacted headquarters. Rather than taking the case to the main police store, it was removed by some Americans who arrived at the farm in a four-wheel-drive vehicle.[15] Police officers involved in searching the area around the farm were briefed that an unnamed young male Arab passenger was suspected of carrying heroin. The Lebanese-American Khaled Jaafar was the only such passenger on the flight (see Chapter 2).[16] Another package of white powder was found on Lockerbie golf course on the night of the disaster.[17] The British authorities have denied that any drugs, other than a personal amount of cannabis, were found at the crash-site.[18]

The authorities also denied that substantial amounts of cash were found. Search volunteers found at least four packages containing very large amounts of US dollars, all of which were handed to the police.[19] Yet, when the issue was raised in parliament, the UK government claimed that nothing other than 'what might ordinarily be regarded as personal money' had been found.[20]

While the Americans at the crash site may have been secretly removing evidence, they may also have been planting it. There is no proof that the CIA, or any other US government agency, deliberately subverted the Lockerbie investigation in order to serve the twin aims of excusing Iran and undermining Libya. However, given their extreme antics during the 1980s, it is by no means absurd to suggest that they did. We now know that the fragment of circuit board, PT/35b, which was the strongest evidential link to Megrahi and the Gadafy regime, could not have originated from one of the 20 timers supplied by Mebo to Libya. The CIA had had an MST-13 since 1986 and knew months before the bombing that the devices had been made by Mebo and supplied to Libya.* Thanks to Majid Giaka, the CIA also knew well before Lockerbie about Megrahi and his movements in and out of Malta. Since it was very likely that Mebo's Edwin Bollier was also reporting back to at least one western intelligence service,† the CIA may also have known before Lockerbie that Megrahi was connected to Mebo via the Libyan company ABH. It is quite possible that the CIA decided to frame Megrahi and worked backwards, planting PT/35b, priming Giaka and leaving the unwitting

---

* This was revealed in Crown precognition statement of a CIA technician who went under the assumed name John Orkin, which was obtained by the Scottish Criminal Cases Review Commission.

† Bollier has never admitted that he was a CIA asset, but when interviewed by the BKA on 9 September 1992 he revealed that he was reporting back to the Swiss Federal Police from as early as 1970, when, following a visit to the Stasi's Scientific and Technical Institute, he was contacted by a senior Swiss federal police officer who asked him detailed questions about the trip. In 1999 one of Bollier's former Stasi handlers told the BKA that by 1987 the Stasi was so concerned that he was working for the CIA and BND that it decided gradually to terminate its contact with him.

Scottish police and FBI to piece together a case with the remaining circumstantial evidence.*

Undoubtedly some of the secret American activity at the crash site was focused on the deeply sensitive issue of the hostages held in Lebanon. Three of the flight's passengers, Major Charles McKee, Matthew Gannon and Ronald Lariviere, were returning from Lebanon, where McKee and Gannon had been engaged in a top secret hostage rescue mission. Gannon was a CIA agent and McKee had been seconded to the agency from the Defence Intelligence Agency.

According to police sources, one of McKee's suitcases was found on Carruthers Farm and removed by Americans, who ignored the standard procedures for the recovery and recording of debris. The case was then cleansed of any sensitive contents and placed back on the farmland, where it was later refound by police officers who were unaware that anything was amiss.[21]

On 11 January 1989, SIO John Orr ordered Detective Chief Inspector Jack Baird and Detective Inspector William Williamson to examine McKee's cases and relay to him any items considered to be of 'potential relevance to intelligence matters.'[22] Among the items they found were photos of what appeared to be a Middle Eastern building.[23] During its investigation of Megrahi's case the SCCRC established that Dumfries & Galloway Constabulary's Joint Intelligence Group, whose role it was to liaise with the intelligence services, kept a file, known as File X, which recorded details of McKee's possessions. In a letter to the SCCRC the police admitted: 'It may

---

* A key element in the circumstantial case was that the bomb originated in Malta. The documentary evidence that supposedly 'proved' this did not emerge from Frankfurt Airport until a few months after the bombing. However, according to the memoirs of the former deputy chief of the US State Department's Diplomatic Security Service, Fred Burton, the CIA told him within ten days of the bombing that 'a suspicious bag – a tan hard-shell Samsonite – has been traced to a flight originating in Malta'.

well have been the case that certain items were not recorded in the normal manner to protect American interests but this is purely speculation on my part.'*[24]

The extreme sensitivity surrounding McKee was illustrated by a bizarre episode a few weeks after the bombing. On 1 February 1989, the Edinburgh commercial radio station, Radio Forth, reported McKee's team's presence on the flight and claimed that the bomb had been planted in their luggage. Within an hour two senior Lothian and Borders officers arrived at the station and demanded that the reporter responsible for the story, David Johnston, reveal his source. When he refused, they told him that they could take him immediately to see Prime Minister Margaret Thatcher and that he could reveal the source to her in private. When he again refused, they warned him that he risked being jailed for contempt. Very unusually the case was then sent directly to the Lord Advocate, Lord Fraser of Carmyllie. Three days later, as the story began to attract substantial media interest, Fraser dropped the case.[25]

According to a number of separate media and legal investigations, McKee's presence on the flight was, as Johnston had suggested, no coincidence. The first such investigation was conducted by a New York-based Israeli investigator called Juval Aviv, who was hired by Pan Am's insurers to investigate the bombing. In his report, which was leaked to the media in Autumn 1989, he claimed that the bombers had exploited a CIA-protected heroin-smuggling operation involving passenger Khaled Jaafar, and had switched one of his drug suitcases with one containing a bomb. More controversially, he alleged that a rogue group within the CIA was facilitating the drug shipments as part of a secret deal with Syrian and Iranian-backed groups who were holding American hostages in Lebanon. He claimed that PFLP-GC leader Ahmed Jibril got

* The SCCRC inspected the file and satisfied itself that it contained nothing of relevance to the destruction of PA103.

wind of the drug-smuggling operation and saw that it could be exploited to smuggle a bomb onto a transatlantic flight. According to Aviv, McKee learned of the rogue operation and was returning to Washington to blow the whistle. The most sensational allegation was that the CIA group were aware of both McKee's and Jibril's plans, and let the bombing happen in order to protect their operation and thwart McKee.

There have been other claims that some western intelligence services knew that Pan Am 103 would be bombed. In 1993 the controversial British businessman Tiny Rowland was told by a senior South African government official that a delegation led by the country's foreign minister, Pik Botha, was meant to be on PA103, but swapped to an earlier flight. According to Rowland, the official said that the government had been warned to avoid the flight by a source that 'could not be ignored'.[26]*

Whatever the truth of these stories, the US and British authorities went to extraordinary lengths to discredit them. Aviv was subjected to what appeared to be a coordinated campaign

---

* In 1994 Botha's Private Secretary told Reuters: 'We . . . got to London an hour early and the embassy got us on an earlier flight. When we got to JFK airport a contemporary of mine said, "Thank God you weren't on 103. It crashed over Lockerbie."' However, in a subsequent Parliamentary answer, justice minister Dullah Omar said: 'Shortly before finalising their booking arrangements for Pan Am flight 103 to New York, they learned of an earlier flight from London to New York, namely Pan Am flight 101.'
Former Foreign Office employee and Essex café owner Patrick Haseldine has for 25 years claimed, without evidence, that the bombing was carried out by the South African Bureau of State Security (BOSS) in order to kill the UN Commissioner for Namibia, Bernt Carlsson, who, like Botha's party, was flying to New York for the signing of the Namibia peace accords. In his prolific online writing Haseldine has also claimed that I was employed by BOSS to conceal its role in the bombing, and that members of the campaign group Justice for Megrahi work for MI6. At the time of writing, he is facing legal action for another of his outlandish libels.

to ruin him and his business, which culminated in a fraud charge relating to another of his corporate investigations, this one based in the Caribbean. In a motion to dismiss the case, his lawyer, Gerald Shargel, wrote: 'In all my years of practice, I have never seen the resources of the FBI and the US Attorney's Office devoted to such an insignificant, inconsequential, isolated four-year-old contract matter . . . What in the world is the Government doing sending FBI agents to the Caribbean to interview individuals as having met with Mr Aviv four years ago for a client who paid $20,000 for the work, never complained, [and] did not challenge Mr Aviv's conclusions? . . . We believe that the evidence points to a clear relationship between Mr Aviv's authoring of the Pan Am report and this mail fraud prosecution.' The motion was unsuccessful, but when the case came to court Aviv was found not guilty.

The fraud charges were brought within days of the broadcast premiere of a documentary, *The Maltese Double Cross*, in which Aviv featured. The film was hugely controversial, not only because its conclusions were broadly similar to his report, but also because it was funded by Tiny Rowland, who had substantial business ties to the Libyan government.* Shortly before the broadcast Tam Dalyell MP, who also featured in the film, was asked to meet a US government information agency official called Todd Leventhal, who had the job title Program Officer for Countering Disinformation and Misinformation. Leventhal told him that some of the film's contributors, including Aviv, were 'known fabricators'.[27]

The day before the broadcast the US Embassy in London and the Crown Office issued press packs, which attempted to debunk the film, to every UK and Scottish national newspaper.[28] The British High Commission in Canberra repeated the exercise when the documentary was broadcast by Australia's SBS channel the following week.[29] Documents disclosed under the Freedom of Information Act in 2005 revealed that a

---

* I was a researcher on the film.

High Commission information officer had colluded with rival broadcaster ABC on a spoiler programme in the *Lateline* slot. In a memo to the Foreign and Commonwealth Office's Drugs, International Crime and Terrorism Department the officer boasted: 'I have been an information officer before, but I cannot recall such an effective hatchet job co-ordinated by the FCO. I have to thank *Lateline* (and its professionalism) for delivering the most savage blows, and you and the Information Department for providing the raw material. Please mark this up as a major success in undermining a potentially damaging programme. We are understaffed and overworked, or we would have blown our own trumpet before, without prompting. I'm afraid we just do the essential, which is the demolition job, not the fancy write-ups.'[30]

Hatchet jobs aside, there is no doubt that there was a reluctance on the part of the UK and US governments to see the PFLP-GC and its Iranian and Syrian sponsors blamed for Lockerbie. In the year after the bombing, despite the mass of circumstantial evidence and leaks that suggested PFLP-GC and Iranian culpability, the US and British governments refused to point the finger publicly. When, in March 1989, the British Transport Secretary, Paul Channon, briefed a group of lobby journalists that the case had been solved and arrests were imminent, it was clear that he was referring to the PFLP-GC, yet everyone else in the government kept quiet.*

According to renowned American investigative reporters Jack Anderson and Dale van Atta, at around the time of Channon's briefing, Prime Minister Margaret Thatcher and President George Bush Snr agreed, during a telephone conversation, that the Lockerbie investigation should be toned

---

* At the time Channon was under great pressure following his department's failure to circulate to airlines prior to the bombing full details of a warning concerning the Toshiba bomb made by the PFLP-GC's Marwan Khreesat. The lobby briefing was clearly meant to divert attention from this failure, but backfired badly when the US TV network ABC identified him as the story's source.

down in order to avoid upsetting negotiations with Iranian and Syrian proxies who were holding British and American hostages in Lebanon.[31] According to Channon's replacement as transport secretary, Cecil Parkinson, Thatcher personally vetoed a request by the British Lockerbie victims' relatives, which Parkinson himself supported, for a judicial inquiry into the bombing.[32]

In February 1990 some of the British Lockerbie victims' relatives were invited to London to meet members of the President's Commission on Aviation Security and Terrorism.* Without prompting, a member of the commission took aside Martin Cadman, who had lost his son Bill in the bombing, and told him privately: 'Your government and ours know exactly what happened but they are never going to tell.'[33] Hardly surprising, then, that Thatcher should block an inquiry.

* The commission was established in the wake of the Lockerbie bombing by President George Bush Snr.

The Crown out of Control 7

As Scotland's sole prosecuting authority, the Crown Office is meant to be an impartial guardian of justice. Unfortunately, as the SCCRC report laid bare, it repeatedly obstructed justice by failing in its duty to disclose evidence that was favourable to the accused.* Since Megrahi's case was referred to the appeal court in 2007, it has often appeared desperate to salvage the conviction and its own reputation. Its legal foot-dragging and distorted public statements have brought further shame upon the Scottish criminal justice system.

Following the referral, Megrahi was legally entitled to submit as many grounds of appeal as he wished. His draft grounds, which were lodged with the high court on 21 December 2007, contained more than the six identified by the SCCRC. The day before, however, Crown counsel, Ronnie Clancy QC, announced to the court that the Crown would seek to restrict the grounds to those six, despite there being no Scottish legal precedent for doing so.†

It would be a further ten months before the judges ruled on the matter, rejecting the Crown's arguments. During that time the Crown attempted to prevent disclosure of previously unseen documents and, more surprisingly, argued that Megrahi's

---

* In 1999 the Crown Office adopted the International Association of Prosecutors' Standards of Professional Responsibility and Statement of the Essential Duties and Rights of Prosecutors, which states that prosecutors should 'carry out their functions impartially' and always protect an accused person's right to a fair trial, and in particular 'ensure that evidence favourable to the accused is disclosed in accordance with the law or the requirements of a fair trial'.

† The law has since changed in line with the Crown's demands – see next chapter.

team should be denied what would normally have been routine access to forensic items – and other evidence – that had featured in the original trial. In attempting to block access to the forensic evidence it argued that its forensic case had already been judged to be sound by both the SCCRC and forensic experts instructed by the defence pre-trial.[1] This was wholly misleading, as the SCCRC had only investigated the provenance of a few forensic items and neither it, nor the original defence experts, had considered any of the forensic arguments in the draft grounds of appeal.

Even after the Crown had failed to restrict the scope of the appeal, it was very slow in meeting its disclosure obligations. It was not until December 2008 that it handed over 7,000 police statements, many of which were previously undisclosed,[2] and even then around 400 of those that were supposed to have been included were missing.[3] Further statements were provided during 2009, but by the time Megrahi returned to Libya in August, much material remained undisclosed. This included eight boxes of files from RARDE, which were not handed over until two months after Megrahi's return.

In March 2012, shortly after the publication of my book *Megrahi: You Are My Jury*, with Megrahi's blessing I gave a copy of the SCCRC report to the *Herald* newspaper, which ran consecutive front page spreads on 13 and 14 March; the first highlighting the Crown's failure to disclose important evidence and the second reporting the commission's implicit criticism of the former Lord Advocate Colin Boyd QC. A reliable source told me that the articles caused consternation and panic in the Crown Office. Whether this is true or not, its behaviour became increasingly undignified and divorced from reality. Ten days after the *Herald* articles, its sister paper, the *Sunday Herald*, notified the Crown Office that it would be publishing the report itself. The Crown Office responded by rushing out a press release confirming that it had no objection in principle to the report being published and revealing that the Lord Advocate had that day written to the SCCRC's chief executive, Gerard Sinclair, to inform him that he did not consider it to be in the public interest to prosecute anyone from the SCCRC for releasing the report. The letter seemed designed to encourage the SCCRC to publish the report immediately, in order to draw the sting from the *Sunday Herald*'s exclusive.

The press release crudely spun the SCCRC's findings, stating in a note to editors: 'In the Megrahi case, the Commission was asked to look at more than 40 possible grounds for a referral to the Appeal Court. The Commission rejected the vast majority of these and referred the case to the Appeal Court on six grounds, many of which were inter-related.'[4]

It was highly misleading to describe many of the SCCRC's six grounds of referral as inter-related, as they were, in fact, distinct, and any one of them could potentially have overturned the conviction. Moreover, in highlighting the number of grounds that the commission had rejected, the Crown Office was presenting the case as if it were a rugby match that it had won 40–6, rather than acknowledging that six was a remarkably high number and that most of the grounds reflected badly on its own actions.

Behind the scenes, the Crown Office was priming the *Daily Record* to run a spoiler against the *Sunday Herald*'s scoop. It appeared the following day under the headline *Lockerbie bomber al-Megrahi's appeal had 'more holes than Swiss cheese'*. It opened: 'The Lockerbie bomber's case that he was the victim of a massive miscarriage of justice is "riddled with inconsistencies", the *Daily Record* can reveal. Sources said Abdelbaset al-Megrahi came up with 40 reasons why he was "wrongly convicted". This was whittled down to just six by Scotland's appeals watchdog – which prosecutors were sure they could tear apart. A Crown Office source said: "When you put them under the microscope, his case starts to fall apart even more. They are full of contradictions and do not add up. For instance, he includes assertions that he never visited Malta when, in fact, we know and can prove that he did. His grounds for appeal has more holes than a Swiss cheese." [5]

As the Crown Office well knew, Megrahi's grounds of appeal did not, in fact, assert that he never visited Malta. Moreover, the SCCRC considered all the inconsistencies and contradictions in Megrahi's accounts and concluded that they did not demonstrate his guilt.

On the day the SCCRC report was published, 25 March, the Crown Office issued another press release, which reflected the state of denial into which it had fallen. Nowhere in its 800-plus words did it acknowledge that the SCCRC had referred the case back to the appeal court; indeed readers unfamiliar with the case could be forgiven for thinking that the SCCRC had upheld the conviction. There was no reference to the Crown's withholding of numerous items of important evidence. Neither did it acknowledge that the commission had described former Lord Advocate Colin Boyd QC's assurances to the trial court regarding the Giaka cables as 'difficult to understand'. It instead focused on one of the few crumbs of comfort that the Crown could draw from the SCCRC report: the fact that the commission had found no evidence that police officers, or other investigators were guilty of serious misconduct. In doing so it adopted the time-honoured diversionary tactic of institutions under pressure – blame the media:

We have become very concerned at the drip feeding of selective leaks and partial reporting from parts of the Statement of Reasons over the last few weeks in an attempt to sensationalise aspects of the contents out of context.

Persons referred to in the Statement of Reasons have been asked to respond to these reports without having access to the statement of reasons and this is to be deplored. Further allegations of serious misconduct

have been made in the media against a number of individuals for which the Commission found no evidence.
This is also to be deplored. In fact the Commission
found no basis for concluding that evidence in the case
was fabricated by the police, the Crown, forensic scientists or any other representatives of official bodies
or government agencies.

The statement did not specify the media in which the false
allegations of serious misconduct had been made. The only
original and substantial media coverage of the SCCRC report
during the previous weeks had been my book *Megrahi: You
Are My Jury*, two accompanying TV documentaries and the
Herald articles of 13 and 14 March, some of which I had written. The book and articles made no such allegations and made
clear that the SCCRC had found no evidence of serious misconduct, while neither TV programme covered the issue. In
effect the Crown Office had wrongly implied that the *Herald*
and I had knowingly made untrue and defamatory claims – an
implication that was, in itself, untrue and defamatory.*

Having committed this slur, the statement cherry-picked
the aspects of the SCCRC report that were least damaging to
the Crown Office and least favourable to Megrahi. (As the
statement is the Crown Office's most detailed comment on
the SCCRC report to date, I have responded to it in detail in
appendix 2.)

The most scandalous aspect of the Crown's behaviour was
its failure to follow up the forensic evidence concerning the
circuit board fragment PT/35b, which proved that it could not

---

* I made an official complaint to the Crown Office about the statement. In her response, the Crown Agent, Catherine Dyer wrote: 'It
is clear that the statement refers widely to allegations made in the
media. This was not a reference to your book, nor was it a specific
reference to the *Herald* newspaper articles you refer to.' As Ms Dyer
should know, this would be no defence were I to have brought a libel
action.

have originated from one of the Thüring boards used in the timers supplied by Mebo to Libya (see Chapter 5). The entire Crown case against Megrahi rested on the claim that the fragment was from one of those boards.

The evidence was set out in *Megrahi: You Are My Jury*, which was published at the end of February 2012. At the time of writing, almost a year and a half on, neither the police nor the Crown Office have spoken to metallurgist Dr Jess Cawley and circuit-board manufacturing expert Dr Chris McArdle. Neither have they contacted Thüring's former production manager Urs Bonfadelli.

The Crown Office's reluctance to examine the new forensic evidence is in contrast to its enthusiasm to gather evidence from Libya. It has always insisted that Megrahi and Fhimah did not act alone, and that the case against their Libyan alleged co-conspirators remains open. In 2012 it claimed that Libya's transitional government had confirmed the old regime's and Megrahi's responsibility for the bombing,[6] but, in fact, neither the interim government, nor the subsequently elected one, did any such thing.

It is quite right that the Crown should pursue its investigation in Libya; however, it appears to be getting nowhere. Remarkably, it was not until late February 2013, over 18 months since Gadafy's fall, that the Scottish police were able to visit Tripoli and then only to discuss requests for cooperation.[7]

At the start of the Libyan revolution, in February 2011, the signs for the Crown were hopeful. Within a few days of the uprising, the newly defected justice minister, Mustafa Abdel Jalil, who was soon to become head of Libya's National Transitional Council, declared to the Swedish newspaper *Expressen*: 'I have proof that Gaddafi gave the order on Lockerbie.'[8] Two high-profile defectors also implicated the old regime: ex-interior minister Abdel Fattah Younes (who was later killed by suspicious revolutionaries) and the ex-ambassador to the UN, Abdul Rahman al-Shalgham.

A few days after the *Expressen* interview, Jalil had more to tell the *Sunday Times*. In a front-page article headlined *Lockerbie bomber 'blackmailed Gadaffi for release'* he claimed that Megrahi had blackmailed Gadafy into securing his release by threatening to expose his role in the bombing, and had 'vowed to exact "revenge"' unless he complied. This was both ludicrous and illogical: Gadafy was not one to be blackmailed; moreover, Megrahi depended upon the Libyan government to fund his appeal and look after his family in Tripoli. In any case, it was already accepted internationally that Gadafy was responsible for the bombing, and Libya had paid compensation to the victims. How could Megrahi expose something that had already been officially recognised? And, if he only cared about his freedom, why, after returning to Libya, would he have spent so much of his remaining time helping me to write his biography? Jalil told the *Sunday Times* that Megrahi was not the man who carried out the planning and execution of the bombing, but had helped the bombers.[9] Here, perhaps, was tacit recognition that the evidence against Megrahi was very weak – something that, as justice minister, he very likely knew.

A few weeks after the article, when asked on BBC *Newsnight* what evidence he had of Gadafy's involvement, he could only cite the fact that Gadafy had supported Megrahi and paid for his legal case.[10] This was not even a revelation, let alone evidence. In the two years since then, Jalil has failed to offer anything better.

The ex-interior minister, Younes, was less explicit than Jalil, which was surprising, given that he had been close to Gadafy for 47 years and was described by some as the Colonel's number two. Asked by the BBC's John Simpson if Gadafy had personally ordered the bombing, he replied, 'There is no doubt about it, nothing happens without Gadafy's agreement. I'm certain this was a national governmental decision.'[11] In an online article Simpson claimed that Younes 'maintains that Col Gaddafi was personally responsible for the decision to blow up the Pan Am flight',[12] but in the broadcast section of the interview he appeared to be expressing a firm belief, rather than certain knowledge. Surely, if Gadafy *had* ordered the bombing, Younes must have known all about it.

Shalgam's claim of Libyan involvement was still less credible, as he had previously declared that the country was not responsible for the bombing.[13] No doubt this was why, when questioned by the Arabic newspaper *al-Hayat*, he gave the vague answer: 'The Lockerbie bombing was a complex and tangled operation . . . There was talk at the time of the roles played by states and organisations. Libyan security played a part but I believe it was not a strictly Libyan operation.'[14]

In January 2012, ITV's *Tonight* programme broadcast an interview with Ashur Shamis, described as an adviser to the new Libyan prime minister, who claimed that Gadafy was personally involved in the planning and execution of the bombing. He added: 'Regardless of what Megrahi did or did not do, that [sic] is a small fish. He is an employee of Libyan security, there is no doubt about it – of external security – and if he was told to do something he would have done it.' How could Shamis be so sure? Because Gadafy had paid compensation to the Lockerbie victims' relatives. 'If he had no role, he wouldn't have paid a penny, he wouldn't have paid a penny,' he insisted.[15] This was nonsense, because, as Shamis should have known, the old regime had only paid compensation in order to rid the country of crippling UN sanctions. Shamis was hardly the most reliable of source on information on the Gadafy regime. He had not lived in Libya since 1973 and was one of the founders and leading lights of the CIA-backed National Front for the Salvation of Libya.[16]

In the two years since the Libyan revolution, the only document about Lockerbie publicly to surface from the Gadafy regime's files is a letter from Megrahi to his relative Abdullah Sennoussi in which he proclaimed his innocence and blamed 'the immoral British and American investigators' for his plight.[17] It is, of course, possible that the Scottish police will gain access to genuine and significant evidence of the old regime's involvement in the bombing; however, that seems increasingly unlikely.

Some senior figures in the new Libya, with considerably more knowledge of both the old regime and the Lockerbie case than Shamis, are very sceptical of the official version. One of them, Mohammed al-Alagi, who was the NTC's first interim justice minister, and who was previously involved in Megrahi's case, has stated publicly that Megrahi was innocent.[18] Some are also opposed to reopening the case. In February 2013, following the visit to Tripoli by the Scottish police, Crown Office and FBI, the country's current justice minister Salah al-Marghani told the *Daily Telegraph*: 'The matter was settled with the Gaddafi regime. I am trying to work on the current situation rather than dig into the past.' His deputy, Hameda al-Magery went further, saying: 'Britain and America are asking us to reopen this file. But this is something of the past. This is over. We want to move forward to build a new future and not to look back at Gaddafi's black history. This case was closed and both UK and US governments agreed to this. They had their compensation.' An unnamed Libyan supreme court official told the paper: 'Even if the government did want to open it they would face opposition from the local people. There would be protests in the streets.'[19]

In response to the *Daily Telegraph* article, the Crown Office swiftly issued a press release, which described the discussions with the Libyans as 'positive' and added 'it is hoped there will be further progress as a result.' It confirmed that the Libyan authorities had raised the issue of compensation, and that the joint Scottish-US delegation had reiterated that the investigation 'was focussed on identifying others involved in this act of state sponsored terrorism.' [20]

Neither the British and American government, nor the Lockerbie victims' relatives, have suggested that Libya should pay further compensation for the bombing. Why then did the Libyan government raise the issue? One likely explanation is that they are aware that the Libyan people would consider it grossly unfair if they were to have to pay yet more compensation for a crime that many believe was nothing to do with their country. It is also possible that the government knows there is no evidence against the old regime and has simply invented an excuse that will save it and the British and US authorities the embarrassment of having to say so publicly.

In September 2012 the committee of the campaign group Justice for Megrahi (JFM) wrote in confidence to the Scottish justice secretary Kenny MacAskill formally to lodge six complaints – later expanded to eight – of alleged criminality against certain Crown representatives who were involved in the Lockerbie investigation and prosecution.[21] Most of the allegations concern failings outlined in this book. They remain unproven and the people named are entitled to the presumption of innocence. The Crown Office could have made this point simply and with dignity, but instead it issued another intemperate and misleading press statement. It declared that the allegations were 'without exception, defamatory and entirely unfounded', which was surprising because JFM had submitted them to MacAskill in confidence, and in outline form only. So, not only should the Crown Office not have seen the allegations, but it also lacked the detail necessary to produce an informed response. Regardless of whether criminality could be proved, the allegations were carefully measured and set out in meticulous detail by a group of highly intelligent concerned citizens.

The Crown Office statement continued:

One of the allegations is also deliberately misleading in that it refers to an issue which has already been extensively and fully investigated by the Scottish Criminal Cases Review Commission which concluded there was no basis to refer the issue to the appeal court. A further allegation made in the letter [break in at Heathrow] was fully investigated by the Appeal Court who heard evidence on the matter and concluded that it did not amount to a miscarriage of justice. Furthermore, the SCCRC was also satisfied after full and proper investigation that there was no basis for concluding that evidence in the case was fabricated by the police, the Crown, forensic scientists or any other representatives of official bodies or government agencies. Had the SCCRC considered there to be any evidence of wrongdoing by any individual involved in the trial then it would have featured in their report as a potential ground of appeal and would have been taken up by Megrahi's lawyers in his second appeal.

As the Crown Office well knew, neither the appeal court nor the SCCRC was tasked with investigating alleged criminality. Furthermore, one of the complaints concerned documents that were unavailable to the SCCRC. The SCCRC did not investigate the specific matters covered by three of the other complaints. The fact that SCCRC had not concluded that evidence was fabricated by anyone involved in the investigation was irrelevant, because none of the complaints alleged such fabrication.

The statement's most remarkable claim was that the JFM committee had been deliberately misleading. It echoed the allegation it had made against the *Herald* and me six months earlier – branding its critics *de facto* liars was clearly becoming a habit. In this case, however, the critics included Dr Jim Swire, who lost his daughter in the bombing, former police superintendent Iain McKie and the former Catholic parish priest for Lockerbie, Father Patrick Keegans.

It is safe to assume that the statement received the blessing of the Lord Advocate, Frank Mulholland QC. On the 24th anniversary of the bombing he launched his own personal offensive in an interview in the Scottish edition of *The Times*, under the front page headline *Pro-Megrahi backers flayed*. Described as 'the most detailed rebuttal yet made' against the claims of Megrahi's supporters, it was, in reality, largely a medley of distortions and bluster.

Describing Megrahi's supporters as 'conspiracy theorists', he said claims of Megrahi's and Libya's innocence were 'without foundation'. The article reported that Mulholland had invited in an independent counsel to conduct a review of the evidence, who had also concluded that the conviction was sound. The truth was very different. As Mulholland later revealed in a letter to MSP James Kelly, who had written to him on behalf of his constituent Jo Greenhorn, the independent counsel was in fact brought in by his predecessor as Lord Advocate, Elish Angiolini QC, in 2007 at the time of the SCCRC's referral of the case to the appeal court. The purpose of the review was to establish whether there was anything in the SCCRC report and its appendices that suggested that the Crown should not defend the conviction. Mulholland told Kelly: 'The outcome of the review satisfied me that the Crown had a robust defence to the potential grounds of appeal identified by the SCCRC.'[22] This did not mean that the independent counsel had concluded that the conviction was sound. More importantly, the review had not considered any of the important evidence that had emerged since 2007, in particular the forensic evidence, revealed in *Megrahi: You Are My Jury*, which proved that the fragment of circuit board, PT/35b, could not have originated from one of the Mebo timers supplied to Libya. The article said that Mulholland had considered 'all the claims advanced in the book' and 'finds no evidence to support them'. As well as being defamatory – implying, once again, that I was guilty of poor journalism – the claim was bizarre, as the book's key claims were based on the testimony of Crown witnesses and on documentary evidence supplied to Megrahi's lawyers by Mulholland's own Crown Office.

In a clear reference to the JFM committee's complaints of alleged criminal misconduct, the article said Mulholland condemned '"defamatory" comments against High Court judges who are unable to respond'. Mulholland described himself as 'hugely frustrated' at 'an unfounded attack on the integrity of the judges involved in the process'. In fact none of the committee's complaints had concerned the judges who heard the case. The only judge Mulholland named was one of his predecessors as Lord Advocate, Colin Boyd QC, who had since been elevated to the bench: 'I saw a report on the BBC that [claimed] a high court judge — Colin Boyd, Lord Advocate at the time — perverted the course of justice. And it frustrates me that they're not in a position to answer these allegations, these can be made without being challenged and without any real foundation.' As Mulholland should have known, the BBC report was wrong, as none of the committee's complaints had concerned Boyd.

He insisted: 'The appropriate place for voicing any concerns about the evidence is before a court of law, not in the court of public opinion, or the media.' Setting aside the irony of this statement (why give a newspaper interview if not to influence the court of public opinion?) it overlooked the fact that the committee's aim was to hold the Crown to account, not to retry Megrahi. The committee had taken the only legal routes that were practically available to have their concerns addressed in a judicial forum: petitioning the Scottish Parliament and complaining to the justice minister Kenny MacAskill and the police. The group only made the complaints public after MacAskill palmed them off onto the police.

Mulholland also gave a distorted account of Megrahi's abandoned second appeal, claiming: 'The [SCCRC] had access to all the Crown's papers, and they took the view that in relation to a very limited number of grounds, the case should be referred back to the appeal court, which they did. The defence were entitled to expand the appeal beyond the grounds of referral, and they included a number of grounds which had been rejected by the commission, and the court was in the process of hearing that appeal when al-Megrahi abandoned his appeal.'

Although in theory the SCCRC had access to all the Crown's papers, its investigation left many key areas of the case, such as the events at Luqa, Frankfurt and Heathrow airports, untouched. As Mulholland should have known, the commission also missed important evidence, including the fact that PT/35b could not have originated from one of the Mebo timers supplied to Libya. In claiming that the commission's grounds were 'very limited' he appeared to be resurrecting the rugby score argument. As he was surely aware, the fact that the commission had found six grounds for referring the case was, in the eyes of most informed observers, remarkable. As in the previous Crown Office statements, he failed to acknowledge that most of the six grounds concerned the Crown's failure to disclose exculpatory evidence.

It was, perhaps, no coincidence that Mulholland granted the interview to *Times* columnist Magnus Linklater. Once an astute commentator on Lockerbie, this pillar of the Scottish press had metamorphosed into the harrumpher-in-chief of the country's 'It-couldn't-happen-here' tendency, and shared Mulholland's tendency to dismiss Megrahi's supporters as conspiracy theorists. A few months earlier he had written a misleading column in response to an Edinburgh International Book Festival event at which Dr Swire, UN trial observer Professor Hans Köchler and I spoke. In it he wrongly accused the three of us of alleging a grand conspiracy to frame Libya involving 'the planting or suppression of forensic evidence, the control of witnesses by intelligence services, the approval of senior politicians, the complicity of police officers, a prosecution team prepared to bend every rule to secure a conviction, and a set of senior Scottish judges willing to go along with

that.' Had he properly read *Megrahi: You Are My Jury*, he
would have known that I did no such thing.*

It is hard to imagine the Director of Public Prosecutions,
who is the chief prosecutor for England and Wales, making
such slanted and inaccurate comments as the Lord Advocate.
Similarly, the Crown Prosecution Service, which the DPP
heads, does not indulge in the type of propagandising and spin
practised by the Crown Office. As the next chapter explains,
the fact that such behaviour has continued unchecked is because the Scottish government has turned a blind eye.

* In a response to Linklater's column, which *The Times* did not publish, I wrote:

> Like the majority of Mr Linklater's fellow audience mem-
> bers on Saturday, I have not swallowed a crazy conspiracy
> theory about Mr Megrahi's conviction. Rather I have noted,
> among other things, that the Crown failed to disclose to
> Mr Megrahi's defence team at least seven key items of ex-
> culpatory evidence; that two of the most important Crown
> witnesses were secretly paid millions of dollars by the US
> Government; and that the trial court's judgment was, ac-
> cording to no less an authority than the Scottish Criminal
> Cases Review Commission, *unreasonable*. All these facts Mr
> Linklater's article omits to mention.
>
> If Megrahi was framed – a big 'if', but not inconceivable
> given their extraordinary antics in the 1980s – it would al-
> most certainly have been done by one of the US intelligence
> services, without the knowledge of the other protagonists
> listed by Mr Linklater . . . [In] my view Mr Megrahi was
> convicted, not because of a grand conspiracy, but, primarily,
> because the police, Crown and judges, while no doubt all act-
> ing in good faith, failed to pursue the truth objectively. It's a
> flaw to which newspaper columnists are equally vulnerable.

A Failure of Politics 8

The *Sunday Herald*'s publication of the SCCRC report on 25 March 2012 subjected the Scottish criminal justice system to one of its greatest ever humiliations. The Commission, remember, had found no fewer than six reasons why Britain's biggest ever criminal case may have resulted in a miscarriage of justice. One of those grounds, remarkably, was that the guilty verdict was, 'at least arguably, one which no reasonable court, properly directed, could have returned.' Given that the court, in this case, was not a lay jury, but three of Scotland's most senior law lords, this was a stunning rebuke. Furthermore, in adding: 'The Commission does not consider there to be any reasonable basis for the trial court's conclusion that the purchase took place on 7 December 1988 and therefore for the inference it drew that the applicant was the purchaser of the items from Mary's House', the SCCRC had come as close as it legally could to saying that it considered, not only the judgment to be unreasonable, but also the guilty verdict itself.

Equally damaging were the SCCRC's findings concerning the Crown. Four of the six appeal referral grounds related to the non-disclosure of potentially vital evidence, and the report revealed numerous other important undisclosed documents.

Until that point there were only a few copies of the report in existence. The question of whether it should be published had become increasingly vexed. Within weeks of Megrahi's return to Libya, the Scottish government claimed that it supported publication, but its behaviour over the following two and a half years suggested that its true intention was to keep the document buried for as long as possible.

In December 2009 justice secretary Kenny MacAskill signed a statutory instrument requiring all those who had supplied information to the SCCRC to consent to its release.[1] The government then claimed that primary legislation was needed to remove the requirement, when in reality all that was necessary was another statutory instrument. It also misleadingly claimed that publication would be subject to data protection restrictions.[2] In fact, the Criminal Procedure (Scotland) Act 1995 specifically provided that, where the disclosure of SCCRC material was permitted by a statutory instrument, no such restrictions applied. Even if the Data Protection Act had applied, anyone with a working knowledge of the Act could have redacted the report to make its publication compliant with the Act.*

The government's reaction to the report's surprise publication was remarkable: it did nothing. Well, almost nothing. It ignored the report's devastating implications for the Scottish criminal justice system and, like the Crown Office, acted as if nothing was amiss. Alex Salmond dutifully echoed the Crown Office's rugby score argument, declaring: 'While the report shows that there were six grounds on which it believed a miscarriage of justice may have occurred, it also rejected 45 of the 48 grounds submitted by Megrahi, and in particular it upheld the forensic basis of the case leading to Malta and to Libyan involvement'. More remarkably, the government went on to state explicitly that it did not doubt the safety of Megrahi's conviction.[3]

In September 2012 I asked the Scottish government whether Salmond and MacAskill had read the report and, if they had, whether it had given the government any concerns about the administration of justice in Scotland?[4] A government official confirmed that MacAskill had read the report and that Salmond had been briefed on its contents. He added: 'It might be helpful for me to clarify Scottish Ministers' position concerning the safety of Mr Al-Megrahi's conviction. Scottish

---

* The *Sunday Herald* published the report with light redactions – most of which were done by me – without falling foul of the Data Protection Act.

Ministers have stated repeatedly their view that as Mr Al-Megrahi was convicted in a court of law, that a court remains the only appropriate forum for considering the evidence and determining his guilt or innocence.'[5] Why, then, I asked, had the government considered it necessary to say that it did not doubt the safety of the conviction, rather than simply stating that it was for the courts to determine its safety?[6] In response, the official could only prevaricate: 'In general terms, in the absence of any court decision quashing a person's conviction, it would not be appropriate for the Scottish Government to call into question the safety of any conviction, which is why it was appropriate for the Scottish Government to state that it did not doubt Mr Al-Megrahi's conviction as the conviction was at the time of such statements (and indeed continues to be) a matter of court record. We have also made clear that a court remains the only appropriate forum for determining Mr Al-Megrahi's guilt or innocence and explained the process by which a further appeal could be heard by the court in this case.'

So, the government did not think it appropriate to call into question the safety of the conviction, but had no qualms about, in effect, calling into question the SCCRC's conclusions and Megrahi's grounds of appeal. It knew very well that Megrahi's family might one day resurrect his appeal and it should also have known well that, in saying that it did not doubt the safety of the conviction it was, in effect, making a public judgement on a process that was supposed to be free from political influence.

It would be surprising if MacAskill, as a former defence lawyer, had not been perturbed by the SCCRC report. He and Salmond claim to favour a public inquiry into Megrahi's case, yet have used spurious excuses to avoid ordering one. When, in September 2010, the Justice for Megrahi group wrote to Salmond to request an independent inquiry, the Scottish government claimed that it lacked the power or remit to institute one.[7] This was nonsense, because Megrahi's conviction and the various controversies surrounding it were, in legal terms, purely Scottish matters, which meant that the government was empowered under the 2005 Inquiries Act. It later admitted this in a letter to the Scottish parliament's public petitions committee,* but then gave a new excuse, namely that 'the wide ranging and international nature of the issues involved' would require the involvement of the UK government. This is thoroughly misleading, because, although an inquiry into the whole of the Lockerbie case would require the co-operation of both governments, the issues of immediate concern were entirely the responsibility of the Scottish criminal justice system. The letter offered the further bogus excuse that Megrahi's guilt or innocence is a matter for the criminal justice system alone to determine. It should have been well aware that the requisite inquiry would be tasked with investigating the conduct of the criminal justice system, not the safety of the conviction.[8]

The latest hopeless excuse came in a June 2013 letter from MacAskill to the Scottish Parliament's justice committee, in which he stated: 'The Scottish Government's position in respect of calls for an independent inquiry is that the matters that an inquiry would look at would be considered appropriately as part of any court appeal that is heard in the Al-Megrahi case.'[9] This was simply untrue, as an appeal would merely challenge the safety of the conviction, and would not answer the key questions about why things went so wrong.

Why is the government so reluctant to confront the scandal of the Megrahi case? The answer, predictably, is politics. Two political factors are especially important. The first is the constitutional peculiarity that means that the country's chief prosecutor and head of the Crown Office, the Lord Advocate,

* The committee was, at the time, considering JFM's petition, which read: 'Calling on the Scottish Parliament to urge the Scottish Government to open an independent inquiry into the 2001 Kamp van Zeist conviction of Abdelbaset Ali Mohmed al-Megrahi for the bombing of Pan Am flight 103 in December 1988.'

is a member of the government. If the government were to admit that the Crown Office had behaved shamefully, it would, in effect, be pointing the finger at one of its own. When it came to power in 2007 the SNP government to some extent depoliticised the Lord Advocate's role, ending the convention that he or she was automatically a member of cabinet; however, he or she still receives all cabinet papers and retains the right to address the cabinet and to attend when required.

A further problem, according to some critics, is the trend in recent years to appoint career prosecutors to the posts of Lord Advocate and Solicitor General.*[10]

Until 2007 both posts were party political appointments. This no doubt helps to explain the shameful silence of the Labour and Conservative parties over the Crown Office's conduct. The Lord Advocate in charge of prosecuting Megrahi and Fhimah, Colin Boyd QC, was appointed by the Labour Scottish Government, while his predecessor, Lord Fraser of Carmyllie, who brought the charges against the two Libyans, was appointed by Prime Minister Margaret Thatcher and also served under her successor, John Major. Boyd, lest we forget, shamefully, if unwittingly, misled the trial court on the matter of the CIA's Giaka cables, while Fraser believed the Crown's star witness, Tony Gauci, to be 'an apple short of a picnic', and should have known that Gauci's clothes purchaser was very different to Megrahi.

It is hardly surprising that the only one of the major parties to be untainted by the Lockerbie prosecution, the Liberal Democrats, is the only one to support a Scottish public inquiry into the affair.[11] The party holds just five of the 129

---

* One such critic, former senior prosecutor Jock Thomson QC, wrote in 2012: 'History will show that the genesis of the destruction of our criminal justice system was the appointment of career prosecutors as law officers. This has led to the unholy, unhealthy alliance of law officers and law makers: MacAskill and Mulholland, in the same bed. There is no separation of powers. Constitutionally, the system now is morally and mortally flawed.'

Scottish parliamentary seats. Of the remaining 124 MSPs, only the SNP's Christine Grahame has consistently raised concerns about the case. Labour, the largest opposition party, has preferred to score cheap political points by berating the government over Megrahi's compassionate release. This demonstrates startling hypocrisy, as it was Tony Blair's Westminster government that negotiated the notorious 2007 'deal in the desert' with Colonel Gadafy, which paved the way for the prisoner transfer agreement that could have allowed Megrahi to be returned to Libya. (In the event he was released on compassionate grounds under entirely different legislation.) Had Labour not lost the Scottish election just a few weeks before the deal was signed, it would almost certainly have allowed Megrahi's return to Libya.

The truth is that Megrahi's terminal cancer provided both the Scottish and UK governments with the get-out that they needed: the Scottish government because it allowed MacAskill to release Megrahi under the existing legal mechanism of compassionate release, rather than one concocted by the hated Westminster, and the UK government because release on compassionate grounds saved the deal in the desert and left MacAskill to take the flak. That, at least, was the theory; in reality the affair massively damaged the Labour government and was hugely uncomfortable for MacAskill and his SNP colleagues.

The second political factor is that the criminal justice system has become a crucial totem in the independence debate. Protecting the reputation of the country's leading independent institution has been essential to the SNP's project, while the unionist parties know that there is nothing to be gained – and, potentially, much to be lost – in criticising that which is most distinctively Scottish.

It is no coincidence that criminal justice has become a key battleground – arguably *the* key battleground – for the SNP government's fights with London; fights that have shown

Salmond and MacAskill at their most aggressive. The fiercest battles have been with the Supreme Court over the key human rights cases of Peter Cadder and Nat Fraser.* In the Cadder judgment of October 2010, the court ruled that the Scottish police practice of interviewing suspects for six hours without a lawyer present breached the European Convention on Human Rights.† In May 2011 the court overturned Fraser's murder conviction, ruling that the Scottish courts had breached his human rights and denied him a fair trial, because, as in the Megrahi case, significant evidence had been withheld.

Rather than acknowledging that the judgments raised serious questions about the quality of Scottish justice, Salmond and MacAskill waged war on the court. Having accused it of 'intervening aggressively' in Scotland's legal affairs, they established an expert legal group to consider how the government could block the court's oversight of criminal cases. Among the measures being considered was a requirement that cases could only be sent to the court by Scottish judges, a process known as certification. Separately, MacAskill ordered a review of whether the Scottish government could withhold its almost half a million pounds annual contribution to the court's costs.[12] He accused the majority of its judges of being ignorant of Scots law and suggested that their knowledge of the country was limited to

* The Supreme Court superseded the Judicial Committee of the House of Lords as the UK's highest court in 2009. Ironically, prior to devolution, Scotland's criminal appeals system was entirely independent of London; however, under the Scotland Act, which established devolution, criminal appeals may be heard in the Supreme Court if the defence believes that there has been a breach of the European Convention on Human Rights, because the UK's human rights regime is a 'reserved', i.e. non-devolved, matter.

† Cadder was convicted in 2009 at Glasgow Sheriff Court of two assaults and a breach of the peace. The conviction was based on a police interview given before his lawyer was present. Until the Supreme Court ruling, the police could question suspects for six hours without a lawyer present.

the Edinburgh Festival.[13] Salmond launched an extraordinary personal attack on Lord Hope, the Supreme Court's presiding Scottish judge in the Fraser case, telling BBC *Newsnight*: 'I don't think it's sensible, fair or reasonable in any jurisdiction where we've a situation where one judge is overruling the opinion of many judges in another court . . . It boils down to the potential replacement of Scottish law by Lord Hope's law. I don't think that's a satisfactory situation.'[14] A fortnight later he intensified the attack, telling *Holyrood* magazine:

> All I would say to Lord Hope is that I probably know a wee bit about the legal system and he probably knows a wee bit about politics but politics and the law inter-twine and the political consequences of Lord Hope's judgments are extreme. And when the citizens of Scot-land understandably vent their fury about the prospect of some of the vilest people on the planet getting lots of money off the public purse, they don't go chapping at Lord Hope's door, they ask their parliament what they are doing about it. I am perfectly happy if Lord Hope wishes to exercise his freedom of speech and I hope he is happy with mine but at least I went to the bother of being elected. It may be an inconvenience but nonetheless it has to count for something.

Salmond used the same interview to launch an equally per-sonal attack on Megrahi's solicitor Tony Kelly, who had won a succession of landmark human rights cases in the House of Lords on behalf of Scottish prisoners.*[15]

A few months later Lord Hope hit back, with rather more finesse, pointing out that the Supreme Court deals with an average of only around two and a half Scottish cases a year,

---

* *Holyrood* magazine deleted defamatory sections of the interview from the online version of the interview after Kelly threatened legal action.

which, as he pointed out was 'not exactly routine interference'. He noted that in England and Wales there was 'none of the feeling of antipathy towards cases being sent to London that lies just below the surface here in Scotland', an antipathy that his fellow Scottish Supreme Court judge, the late Lord Rodger, had put down to 'a corrosive anti-English sentiment'.[16] As all the contentious Scottish human rights cases heard by the Supreme Court have had a Scottish presiding judge, the term 'anti-English' was not strictly accurate. Antediluvian was, perhaps, closer to the mark.

The Megrahi case has far more potential to damage the Scottish criminal justice system than the Cadder and Fraser judgments. This perhaps explains the government's handling of the JFM committee's complaints of alleged criminality. The committee did not make the complaints lightly: having studied the evidence in detail, and having had their calls for a public inquiry repeatedly rebuffed, they felt it was the only way to persuade MacAskill to order an inquiry.

The JFM committee's secretary, Robert Forrester, submitted the allegations to MacAskill on 13 September 2012 in strict confidence, yet the government passed them on to the Crown Office, despite the fact that the complaints named Crown officials. Owing to the gravity of the allegations, the committee requested that MacAskill appoint an independent investigator to examine them, which he was empowered to do under the 2005 Inquiries Act. As a lawyer, he must have known that, although unproven, the complaints were substantial and very serious, yet he refused the request, instead insisting that the committee take them to Dumfries & Galloway Constabulary, even though police officers and other Crown servants were named in some of the complaints.

Although the police appear to be taking the JFM committee's complaints seriously, it is too much to expect both they and the Crown Office (to which they will report) will be completely impartial. If, as seems very likely, no criminal prosecutions arise from the complaints, the government will have a further hollow excuse for not ordering an inquiry.

The government's desire to protect the criminal justice system may also explain why Megrahi dropped his second appeal against conviction prior to being released on compassionate grounds, even though he was not legally required to do so. According to Libyan minister Abdulati al-Obedi, who led negotiations with the Scottish government over Megrahi's release, MacAskill privately indicated to him, after a meeting on 10 August 2009, that it would be easier to grant compassionate release if Megrahi abandoned the appeal.[17] The delegation immediately visited Megrahi in prison and gave him a note of the conversation. It was clear to him that he could not risk continuing with the appeal and the following day he reluctantly told his solicitor Tony Kelly to abandon it.

MacAskill denies Obedi's account and claims that it is refuted by a minute of the meeting made by a civil servant.[18] However, the minute runs to just five short paragraphs and the alleged conversation, which was separate to the main meeting, was only noted by the Libyans. A few days before the meeting, the *Herald* reported: 'Technically [Megrahi] could continue his appeal [if granted compassionate release], but there is a growing expectation that he would be encouraged to first drop legal proceedings.'[19] The source of this information was unclear, but the wording suggested that the tip-off came from the Scottish rather than the Libyan side. The Libyans were not given to non-attributable press briefings; moreover they had nothing to lose if the appeal went ahead, other than Megrahi's legal costs, which were insignificant when compared to the $2.7 billion paid to the Lockerbie victims' relatives in order to rid the country of sanctions. The Scottish government, by contrast, not only feared reputational damage to the criminal justice system, but also knew it would be flayed by the press if Scottish taxpayers had to continue funding the expensive court case while Megrahi was at home in Libya.

Megrahi's family and supporters are entitled to pursue a new appeal via the SCCRC; however, the government has introduced two important legal changes that will make that significantly more difficult. The first of these, which was brought in under the Criminal Justice and Licensing (Scotland) Act 2010, compels appellants whose cases have been referred for appeal by the SCCRC to restrict their grounds of appeal to those identified by the commission, or else seek the high court's leave to expand the grounds within 21 days of the referral. This goes close to what the Crown unsuccessfully argued for at Megrahi's appeal, which strongly suggests that the legislation was conceived in the Crown Office. The change leaves appellants at the mercy of the SCCRC's competence, which, as Megrahi's case illustrates, can vary hugely. While its investigation of the Gauci evidence was impressively thorough, the forensic investigation missed important evidence, including proof that the circuit board fragment PT/35b could not have originated from one of the timers supplied by Mebo to Libya.

The second change was slipped into the Criminal Procedure (Legal Assistance, Detention and Appeals) (Scotland) Act, known as the Cadder emergency legislation, which was passed within days of the Supreme Court's Cadder judgment, without parliamentary scrutiny. The act's main purpose was to enshrine the ruling within Scots law, but section 7 introduced additional tests for cases referred by the SCCRC to the appeal court. It inserted a new clause into the Criminal Procedure (Scotland) Act 1995, requiring the SCCRC to have regard to: 'the need for finality and certainty in the determination of criminal proceedings' when considering whether it was in the interests of justice to refer cases to the appeal court. A further clause was added that required the court to apply the same test before considering cases. In effect, this gave the court a 'gate-keeping' role, which allowed it to dismiss cases referred by the SCCRC without having to go through the process of a full appeal hearing.

The stated intention behind these legislative changes was to prevent a flood of cases being referred for appeal on the basis of the Cadder judgment. The government could have achieved this by focusing the clause narrowly on cases like Cadder's in which appellants had been denied access to a solicitor before making police statements. The vague wording suggested a broader aim of reducing the overall number of appeal referrals by the SCCRC. The implication seemed clear: the commission was not trusted by the appeal court and needed to become more stringent in its criteria for referring cases. The SCCRC's chair, Jean Couper, noted that the legislation had created 'a fundamental constitutional change in the role of the Commission and in its relationship with the appeal court in Scotland.' She said there was no evidence that it was required and no evidence 'of any concern amongst the judiciary that the Commission is unable or unwilling to undertake its duties in a measured, considered and appropriate way.' Following a general review of criminal law and practice by Lord Carloway, the government agreed to scrap the appeal court's gate-keeping role; however, the latest Criminal Justice (Scotland) Bill, published in June 2013, contains a new 'finality and certainty' test, which the court must apply when considering whether to quash convictions.

The two legislative changes place huge pressure on the SCCRC at a time when its resources are being squeezed.* They appear to be nothing more than a land grab by the government to help protect the reputation of the Scottish criminal justice system by reducing the flow of embarrassing miscarriage of justice cases.

If the major parties won't acknowledge the Lockerbie scandal, then who will? The only current hope of progress at Holyrood lies with the Scottish parliament's justice committee, which, at the time of writing, is holding open the Justice

---

* By 2014/15 the Commission's budget will have decreased by 10.6 per cent compared to 2011/12.

for Megrahi group's petition for an independent inquiry into Megrahi's conviction, pending the outcome of the JFM committee's complaints to the police.*

---

* It is also to the credit of the parliament's petitions committee that it referred the case to the justice committee.

Conclusion: A System in Denial

Anyone who doubts that the Scottish criminal justice system, civil servants and politicians will go to extreme lengths to protect themselves, conceal the truth and uphold dubious convictions can be countered with two words: Shirley McKie. For simply standing up for truth and justice, the former Strathclyde Police detective constable and her small band of supporters brought the system to its knees. Her case has startling parallels to Lockerbie and may, indeed, be intimately linked to it.

McKie's story began on 8 January 1997 when retired bank clerk Marion Ross was found murdered in her home in Kilmarnock. It was an especially brutal attack, which suggested that the killer was a sadistic psychopath. Within two weeks the police had their prime suspect. Handyman David Asbury had worked on an extension at Ross's house some years earlier, and subsequent to the murder had become suicidal. Although he did not fit the psychological profile of the murderer, there appeared to be hard evidence against him in the form of two fingerprints, which had been identified by officers from the Scottish Criminal Records Office (SCRO). The first, found on a Christmas gift tag in the murder house, was said to be his, while the second, which was far more damning, was found on a cash-filled tin in his bedroom and was allegedly the victim's.

There was, however, another print, which was clearly not Asbury's; this was found close to Ross's body, halfway up the bathroom doorframe. If the SCRO fingerprint experts had been unable to eliminate it, then the case against Asbury might have been severely weakened. The fingerprints of all the officers who had visited the murder house were provided to the SCRO for analysis. In early February, no doubt to the police's relief, the SCRO reported that the experts had matched one of them, belonging to McKie, with the doorframe print.

When McKie was told of the development, she explained that there must have been a mistake: although she had attended the house on three occasions, she had not entered, because she was not authorised to. Rather than believing her, senior colleagues made it clear that she must 'come clean' and admit that she had been in the house. When she refused, she triggered an astonishing decade-long campaign of bullying, smears and official stonewalling, which drove her to the brink of suicide, and shattered public faith in Scottish criminal justice.

When Asbury's case came to trial McKie was reluctantly called as a defence witness. She knew that if the jury believed her then they might accept that the SCRO officers had misidentified all the fingerprints, in which case Asbury – whom she then believed to be guilty – might walk free. Unfortunately, in the absence of any scientific challenge to the fingerprint evidence, the Crown successfully portrayed her as a liar and Asbury was convicted.

A few months later McKie was arrested in a dawn raid, taken to Ayr police station and charged with perjury. The event was clearly orchestrated in order to compound her already extreme distress. She was strip-searched – a humiliating ordeal that is usually reserved for suspected drug dealers and violent criminals – and taken to Glasgow, where she was locked up in a police cell.

That the police and Crown ever pursued the case is astonishing. None of the officers who were on duty at Ross's house said that she had been inside, and their accounts were supported by the crime scene logs. Moreover, forensic evidence, which the defence only learned of during the course of McKie's trial, showed that the disputed fingerprint must have been made before 10 January, yet the Crown case was that she had been in the house after that date. Equally shockingly, Strathclyde Police's chief medical officer failed to disclose a

1997 psychological assessment report, which the force had commissioned from leading clinical psychologist Professor Colin Espie, in which he clearly stated that she appeared to be telling the truth.

The Crown case rested almost entirely upon the evidence of the four SCRO experts who had supposedly matched McKie's fingerprint to the one on the bathroom doorframe. What the Crown failed to reveal is that the four's work had been 'blind tested' by five of their colleagues, none of whom had been able to make to make a full identification of McKie's print.

Three of the original four experts – Charles Stewart, Hugh Macpherson and Fiona McBride – gave evidence at McKie's trial. Each staunchly maintained that the doorframe print was McKie's. However, their claims were comprehensively destroyed by two far better qualified American experts called by the defence. Pat Wertheim and David Grieve were both certain that the print was not McKie's and were able to demonstrate their claims with relative ease. The jury was out for less than 90 minutes before unanimously finding McKie not guilty. It was the first time that Crown fingerprint evidence had been successfully challenged in a Scottish criminal trial. Clearly perturbed by the case, the judge, Lord Johnston, told her: '[I]t's not appropriate for me to comment on the jury's verdict, nor to comment upon how you find yourself in the situation you have found yourself in, but personally I would like to extend to you my respect for the obvious courage and dignity with which you have shown throughout this nightmare, as you've described it. I very much hope you can put it behind you. I wish you all the best.' Remarkably, even the Advocate Depute, Sean Murphy QC, privately wished her good luck.

The acquittal should have prompted the SCRO, police and Crown to admit their mistakes, apologise to McKie and urgently review fingerprinting procedures. To have done so, of course, would not only have severely damaged their reputations, but might also have prompted a flood of appeals against convictions based upon fingerprint evidence. Instead they battened down the hatches and hoped that the issue would go away. It didn't: not only did a growing chorus of international experts condemn the SCRO's work, but, remarkably, so too did 14 experts from the Lothian & Borders Police fingerprint bureau in Edinburgh, and later some of their peers from the Grampian Police bureau in Aberdeen. In a letter sent to the Lord Advocate Andrew Hardie and the justice minister Jim Wallace on 26 January 2000, the Edinburgh experts wrote: 'At best the apparent "misidentification" [of the fingerprints] is a display of gross incompetence by not one, but several experts within that bureau. At worst it bears all the hallmarks of a conspiracy of a nature unparalleled in the history of fingerprints.'

In the face of a growing campaign by the McKies and a BBC TV documentary *Finger of Suspicion*, the authorities could no longer afford to be seen to do nothing. In February, following a unanimous decision by the Association of Chief Police Officers of Scotland (ACPOS), the SCRO's executive committee invited Her Majesty's Chief Inspector of Constabulary, William Taylor, to conduct an independent assessment of the evidence used against McKie. Taylor instructed two foreign experts to examine the fingerprints: Arie Zeelenberg, head of the Netherlands National Fingerprint Unit, and Torger Rudrud, a Norwegian assistant chief constable. Both agreed that the doorframe print was not McKie's. The finding prompted ACPOS's president, Chief Constable Willie Rae, to apologise to McKie. When the inquiry results were announced to the Scottish Parliament in June 2000, Hardie's successor as Lord Advocate, Colin Boyd, announced that in future all cases involving SCRO fingerprint evidence would be subjected to external checks by an outside fingerprint bureau.

Only the following month, following a series of media revelations and the formal submission of criminal allegations against the SCRO experts by McKie's father Iain, did the Lord

Advocate see fit to instigate an investigation into possible criminal conduct by Strathclyde Police and the SCRO. The Paisley procurator fiscal, William Gilchrist, appointed Tayside police deputy chief constable James Mackay and Detective Chief Superintendent Scott Robertson to lead the investigation. Their report, delivered later that year, was devastating: they had found evidence of 'cover-up and criminality' and 'collective and cultural collusion' among SCRO staff. Yet, to Mackay's surprise and disappointment, Boyd opted not to launch prosecutions. The four SCRO experts responsible for matching McKie's print were instead suspended pending a wholly inadequate disciplinary inquiry, which, unsurprisingly, exonerated them.

It was, at least, clear that David Asbury's conviction was wholly unsafe. In August 2000 he was granted interim liberation and two years later his conviction was formally quashed. However, little else changed. The SCRO and police failed to acknowledge their mistakes, even though many SCRO staff and rank and file police officers were appalled by McKie's treatment. Faced with overwhelming evidence of her innocence, certain officers resorted to spreading false rumours that McKie was known to have lied in order to conceal a sexual relationship with another officer.

The Scottish Government (then known as the Scottish Executive) was little better. It was well aware of Mackay's findings, but instead of launching a full inquiry and offering McKie an apology and compensation, it perpetuated the fiction that she had fallen victim to an honest mistake rather than a noxious brew of institutional incompetence, bullying and cover-up. No doubt part of the reason was that she had, by then, begun a civil action against the government. The stonewalling continued until 2006 when, on the day McKie's case was due to be heard, the government made an out of court settlement for £750,000 plus legal expenses, but with no apology. It emerged that in 2004 the government had commissioned independent expert John Macleod to review the fingerprint evidence. He too was clear that the doorframe print was not McKie's; yet the government buried his report and failed to settle the case for a further two years, despite being well aware of the severe trauma that it was causing McKie.

It was not until 2008 that the recently installed SNP government ordered an inquiry into the case, but its terms of reference were limited to consideration of the fingerprint evidence, rather than the wider cover-up and the campaign against McKie. Although she was once again exonerated, the Scottish criminal justice system and those responsible for her plight were left relatively unscathed. Finally, in 2011, justice secretary Kenny MacAskill formally apologised to McKie for her treatment. Welcome though this was, more than 16 years since her ordeal began, none of those responsible have been properly held to account.

Perhaps the most shocking aspect of the police's and SCRO's conduct is that it may well have allowed Marion Ross's killer to strike again. In 2005, when studying a leaked police log, Iain McKie discovered that only a fortnight after the murder a well-known local violent criminal Patrick Docherty was 'alleged to have made remarks to previously reliable informant that he was involved in the crime'. In 2003 Docherty and an accomplice broke into the house of 91-year-old Margaret Irvine, who lived just a few miles from Marion Ross, and murdered her in similarly brutal fashion. Iain McKie believes that this could explain why the police failed to reinvestigate the Ross murder. Had they done so, the trail might well have led to Docherty, in which case they might have had to acknowledge that their earlier mistakes had cost the life of Margaret Irvine.

Although, to the best of our knowledge, no one involved in the Lockerbie investigation was persecuted as Shirley McKie was, there are numerous clear parallels with Lockerbie: the wrong person was convicted on the basis of highly flawed evidence; the real killers remained free; vital exculpatory evidence was concealed; the agencies responsible remained in denial about their failings; and, thanks to the Scottish government's failure honestly to address the scandal, none of those responsible have been properly held to account. Why so many parallels? Because the Lockerbie investigation and trial was conducted under a system that, as McKie learned to her cost, was capable of going to any lengths to prevent the truth and its own shortcomings ever being revealed.

There are not only numerous similarities to Lockerbie; there may well be a direct link. James Mackay delivered his interim report on the McKie case, which suggested that there had been a criminal cover-up, in August 2000 in the middle of Megrahi and Fhimah's trial. The Lord Advocate Colin Boyd QC took his decision not to prosecute the SCRO officers named in Mackay's final report in 2001, when the Crown Office was bracing itself for Megrahi's first appeal against conviction. Although the SCRO was not centrally involved in the Lockerbie case, charges against its officers would have cast grave doubt upon the probity of Scottish criminal investigations in general and of Scottish forensic science in particular. Iain McKie and a number of close observers of his daughter's case, including a very senior government politician, believe that the Crown Office could not allow this to happen.

Furthermore, the head of the SCRO throughout much of the McKie scandal was Harry Bell, who, as head of the Maltese investigation, was the single most important detective in the Lockerbie case. The chief constable of Strathclyde Police, who bore ultimate responsibility for the Asbury and McKie investigations, was Sir John Orr, who was the senior investigating officer in charge if the Lockerbie inquiry for the first 12 months after the bombing.

The two American fingerprint experts instructed by McKie's defence team, Pat Wertheim and David Grieve, both found themselves under pressure from the FBI over their involvement in the case. Grieve described in an email to Iain

McKie how, prior to the publication of an editorial critical of the Crown's fingerprint evidence, which he had written for the *Journal of Forensic Identification*, he 'was asked by a very high ranking person of the FBI not to publish anything about the case'. Shortly before, the FBI had warned him not to embarrass a 'sister agency' that had pending 'very important and high-profile cases' of international significance. Although Lockerbie was not named, it was obvious to Grieve that it was this to which the FBI was referring.[1]

Like the McKie and Asbury cases, there is overwhelming evidence that the Lockerbie investigation, and the subsequent prosecution and conviction of Abdelbaset al-Megrahi, went terribly awry. Although it might have been impossible to acquire proof of who carried out the bombing, once the police had their supposedly hard evidence against him and Fhimah, the trail to the PFLP-GC and Iran was allowed to go cold. As a consequence, 25 years after the bombings we are no closer to knowing exactly who ordered and carried out the attack than we were a year after it.

The hard evidence against the Libyans proved to be anything but. Documents from Luqa airport severely undermined the Malta bomb theory, which depended upon far less reliable documents from Frankfurt airport. The identification evidence was extremely shaky and came courtesy of a witness whom the Lord Advocate responsible for charging the Libyans described as 'an apple short of a picnic', and who knew that he stood to earn a substantial reward. Another key witness was a dodgy CIA informant, who also made millions. Worse still, the police failed to pursue evidence that the circuit board fragment PT/35b was different to the Thüring boards used in the timers supplied to Libya.

The Crown concealed crucial evidence from the defence both before and after the trial, including the documents concerning the Gauci brothers' interest in rewards, and test results indicating that Allen Feraday was aware that PT/35b was different to a control sample Thüring circuit board. At trial two senior prosecutors, Norman McFadyen and Alan Turnbull QC, secretly viewed previous unredacted CIA cables concerning Majid Giaka and convinced themselves that they were not relevant to the Libyans' defence, when, in reality, the opposite was true.

The Crown case fell far short of proof, but the judges made up for some of its shortcomings, most notably by convicting Megrahi and acquitting Fhimah, in apparent contradiction of the Crown's claim that they must have acted together. They had no doubt that Megrahi was the bomber despite the evidence from Luqa, the faulty identification, and the meteorological data that all but ruled out 7 December – Megrahi's only window of opportunity – as the clothing purchase date.

The SCCRC went as close as it legally could to saying that the verdict was unreasonable, and found no fewer than six grounds for referring the case for appeal. By any measure, this was a humiliating rebuke, yet the Crown Office's responses have ranged from petty indignation to misleading spin. It appears to be sticking its fingers in its ears and shouting to drown out the sound of the conviction crumbling around its feet.

The Crown Office must be desperately hoping that new evidence will emerge from Libya, but, two years on from Gadafy's fall, nothing credible has publicly surfaced to suggest that his regime was behind the bombing, let alone that Megrahi was involved. It is likely that the police, Crown Office and Scottish government will eventually have to acknowledge that the investigation there has proved fruitless.

In the meantime the government is clinging to the fiction that the investigation, prosecution and conviction were all sound. The shameful hollowness of this position was exposed by Kenny MacAskill's handling of the Justice for Megrahi committee's complaints of criminal misconduct. He knew that, by refusing to appoint an independent figure to investigate them, he had left the committee with no choice but to submit them to the very police force that was the subject of some of the complaints. He also knows that a police investigation is no substitute for a public inquiry, because the key question to be answered is not *Was there criminal misconduct?* but, rather, *Why did things go so wrong?*

When in opposition, Alex Salmond said that the Shirley McKie case had exposed 'a responsibility vacuum at the top' of the Scottish Government, and that the issues it raised went 'right to the heart of the justice system in Scotland' and were 'ten times as important to the future of Scotland' than those that led to the inquiry into the overspend on the Scottish Parliament building. He added: 'The First Minister cannot seriously believe a few flimsy words can divert us from a full and proper investigation into the scandal.'[2] Lockerbie is far more important than the McKie case, so why was Salmond's government prepared to order an inquiry into McKie's case – albeit an overly restricted one – yet will only offer 'a few flimsy words' on Megrahi's? The likely answer is that, whereas the McKie inquiry reflected well on the SNP government and had negative repercussions only for the SCRO, a Megrahi inquiry – given proper terms of reference – would implicate successive governments and endanger the reputation of the entire criminal justice system. The Labour and Conservative parties have also turned their back on the scandal. Scottish criminal justice is highly politicised, and no case, including Shirley McKie's, has had more potential to cause political damage than Megrahi's. The SNP government cannot concede that the country's foremost independent institution could fail so badly, while Labour and the Tories are reluctant to confront the scandal, not least because to do so would highlight their own failures. As long as the collective state of denial persists, the Crown Office can be confident of escaping censure.

The Scottish government has privately suggested that it favours an appeal followed by an inquiry, but this is simply another means of delaying an inquiry. It knows that the Megrahi family's precarious position in Libya makes it difficult for them to pursue an appeal. Even if they were able to, the time interval between them applying to the SCCRC and an appeal being completed would be years.

It is to be hoped that Megrahi's conviction is one day over-turned, but clearing his name is not enough. For the stain of Lockerbie to be erased there must be a public inquiry that holds the police, Crown Office and prosecutors to account. At a minimum it should consider:

- What other potentially helpful evidence was withheld from the defence.
- Why such evidence was not disclosed.
- Why charges were brought against the two Libyans when it was clear that the key evidence was highly unreliable.
- Why important leads were not pursued.
- What potentially important evidence was lost and why.

Ideally the inquiry should also consider aspects of the case that are outside the Scottish government's jurisdiction, most importantly:

- The warnings that were received before the bombing.
- What the UK government knew about the attack and what, if any, influence it had on the investigation.
- The role of the intelligence services in the investigation.
- The role of the US agencies at the crash site and in the wider inquiry.
- The evidence against the alternative suspects.

The Scottish government has nothing to lose by extending the inquiry in this way: if the UK and US governments refuse to cooperate, their evasion will be clear to all.

Lockerbie is about more than an unsolved crime and a gross miscarriage of justice: it is about trust in public institutions. Injustice is uniquely toxic to that trust. By failing to recognise and address the injustice, the Crown Office and government have themselves becomes toxic; not only to those, like my friend Jim Swire, who were directly affected by the bombing, but to everyone who cares about truth, openness and accountability in public life. Whether the country remains devolved or becomes independent, its leaders must face this reality. If they continue to look the other way, they will shame Scotland for generations to come.

Appendix 1

The Official Response to the New Forensic Evidence Concerning Circuit Board Fragment PT/35b

In February 2012 the producers of a BBC TV documentary asked RARDE's successor organisation, the Defence Science and Technology Laboratory (DSTL): 'How does [DSTL] explain the difference in the ratio of lead to tin between the MEBO timers and the fragment found? The MEBO timers being approximately a 70% to 30% tin/lead alloy and the fragment effectively being pure tin. (I refer you to the memos written by Allen Feraday enclosed).'*

DSTL's reply, which was very likely prepared in consultation with the Crown Office, went as follows:

> The memos specified refer to the timer fragment found by Dr. Hayes, and only one specific MEBO MST-13 timer (DP/347(a)). The fragment tracks are copper with a coating of pure tin. Mr. Feraday specifically notes that although the tracks on the one board noted here have a coating of lead and tin, it is quite possible that this has been added (by dipping or rolling) over the top of a track of copper coated with pure tin. In Mr. Feraday's examination notes of another MEBO MST-13 timer board (DP/111), he specifically notes that the tracks are of copper with a coating of pure tin. The point is that the identification of the fragment as originating from a MEBO MST-13 timer board is based on comparing the tracking pattern, materials and construction of several such timer boards with the fragment. The control samples supplied came in a variety of configurations. The fact that one might have had a modified or added coating on some of its tracks does not detract from the identification of the fragment as originating from a board with the same master tracking pattern as, and thus one variety of, the MEBO MST-13 timer board.

* The memos referred to are the metallurgy tests results dated 1 August 1991, in which Feraday noted that difference in the plating between PT/35b and DP/347a.

135

The response, at first glance, seemed plausible, but, when considered in the context of other available evidence, proved to be fallacious. DP/347a was one of four identical circuit boards, which were collectively numbered DP/347. When describing DP/347, both in his forensic report and at trial, Feraday said: 'All four circuit boards are essentially similar in tracking pattern, colour and materials to the green coloured control panels/circuit boards present upon the three "MST-13" control sample timers described above as DP/111, DP/84 and DP/100.'

DP/111 was not, as the DSTL statement implied, a circuit board, but was rather, as Feraday indicated, a complete control sample timer containing a circuit board. Both it and the other control sample, DP/100, were made especially for the police by Mebo using boards that were left over from the original Thüring order. Feraday was perhaps unaware that all the boards in RARDE's possession originated from Thüring. The company's production records demonstrated that the boards came in only two configurations: the first were coated with a resin-like substance called solder mask on the reverse side to the circuitry, and the second were solder-masked on both sides. As Thüring's production manager, Urs Bonfadelli, confirmed, the plating on both varieties was a tin-lead alloy. It therefore stood to reason that Feraday's examination notes were wrong in claiming that DP/111's board was plated with pure tin. Furthermore, there were no test results to indicate that DP/111 had been subjected to metallurgy tests. This is not surprising, because, as it was built into a functioning timer, it would have been difficult to fit it within the testing equipment without disassembling the timer. The examination notes, which were dated 4 July 1991, stated: 'The precise copper tracking pattern present upon the underside of the circuit board [of DP/111] is surface coated with a layer of pure tin'. A month after making the notes, on 1 August 1991, Feraday oversaw the metallurgy tests on DP/347a, which confirmed that it was plated with tin-lead alloy. The forensic report, which he completed in December 1991, said of DP/111's board only 'the precise pattern of conducting tracks are etched on to the underside' but, significantly, made no mention of pure tin plating, perhaps because Feraday had deduced from the 1 August tests on DP/347a that its plating was not pure tin.

If in the very unlikely event that DP/111's board *had* been plated with pure tin, then Feraday, as an electronics expert, should have known that it was significant and noted the dissimilarity between it and DP/347a; however, he did not.

When describing PT/35b, Feraday stated in his report and at trial:

> The particular tracking pattern of the fragment has been extensively compared with the control samples of the "MST-13" timers and circuitboards (items DP/111, DP/84, DP/100 and DP/347(a)), and it has been conclusively established that the fragment materials and tracking pattern are similar in all respects to the area around the connection pad for the output relay of the "MST-13" timer. This particular area on the control sample "MST-13" circuitboard (item DP/347(a)) is shown in photograph 335 at approximately the same degree of magnification (x15) as the previous photograph (334) of the fragment PT/35(b). A direct comparison between the fragment PT/35(b) and the control sample circuitboard ((DP/347(a)) is shown in photograph 336 wherein the section DP/31, which was removed from the fragment for investigational purposes, is included. The conducting pad and tracks present on the fragment PT/35(b) are of copper covered by a layer of pure tin.

This clearly implied that DP/347a, as well as the boards in the control sample timers DP/111, DP/100 and DP/84, were coated with pure tin, yet, months before completing the report, Feraday had overseen the tests that proved that DP/347a was plated with a tin-lead alloy; indeed, he was sufficiently struck by the plating to attempt, in his handwritten notation, an explanation for it – the explanation being that the alloy had been added on top of a layer of pure tin. Thüring's method of production did not involve a tin-lead alloy being laid upon a layer of pure tin and the electronics experts I have consulted are not aware of circuit boards ever having been plated in this way. Feraday was apparently trying to explain why PT/35b could have been plated with pure tin and DP/347a plated with tin-lead. He perhaps thought it possible that the heat of the explosion could have removed the layer of tin-lead from the fragment and exposed a layer of pure tin underneath. However, if the tin-lead had been removed, then so too would a blob of tin-lead solder, which had obviously been used to attach a component to the circuitry, and which was still clearly visible on the fragment.

Appendix 2

Author's Response to Crown Office Statement of 25 March 2012

The statement is in italics, with my comments in normal typeface. My observations on the first two paragraphs are in Chapter 7.

We have become very concerned at the drip feeding of selective leaks and partial reporting from parts of the Statement of Reasons over the last few weeks in an attempt to sensationalise aspects of the contents out of context.

Persons referred to in the Statement of Reasons have been asked to respond to these reports without having access to the statement of reasons and this is to be deplored. Further allegations of serious misconduct have been made in the media against a number of individuals for which the Commission found no evidence. This is also to be deplored. In fact the Commission found no basis for concluding that evidence in the case was fabricated by the police, the Crown, forensic scientists or any other representatives of official bodies or government agencies.

1. *The SCCRC found nothing to undermine the trial court's conclusions about the timer fragment, namely that it was part of a timer manufactured by a Swiss company, MEBO, to the order of the Libyan intelligence services.*

The SCCRC missed the fact that the circuit board fragment, PT/35b, could not have been from one of the timers sold by Mebo to Libya. (See chapter 5).

2. *The SCCRC report confirms that Tony Gauci was paid a reward by US authorities only after the first appeal.*

This overlooked the fact that: a) Gauci expressed an interest in being rewarded before his original tentative identification of Megrahi; b) he was under the influence of his brother Paul who repeatedly raised the issue of rewards with the police; c) Tony and Paul were respectively paid at least $2 million and $1 million. The fact that they were not paid until after the first appeal was irrelevant, as it was their expectation of being rewarded that was key.

3. *No inducements or promises of reward were made by US and Scottish Law enforcement prior to his evidence being given.*

This missed the fact set out under point 2, above. Furthermore, according to DCI Harry Bell's diary, on 28 September 1989, FBI agent Chris Murray told Bell that he (Murray): 'had the authority to arrange unlimited money for Tony Gauci and relocation is available. Murray states that he could arrange $10,000 immediately.' Murray would not have said those things unless he believed that the offer might have been put to Gauci. According to the head of the FBI investigation, Richard Marquise, 'everybody that [sic] worked for me were under orders that they were not allowed to tell people that they could get money for this case.'[1] This begged the question, was Murray acting against Marquise's orders?

4. *At no stage was he offered any inducement or reward by Scottish authorities who acted with complete propriety throughout the case.*

Again, see 2 above. Furthermore, in a letter to the US Department of Justice, written a month after Megrahi's failed first appeal, the Scottish police's senior investigating officer wrote to the US Department of Justice asking that Tony Gauci be paid at least $2 million and Paul at least $1 million. The letter acknowledged that the Crown Office was prevented by its own rules from seeking a reward, but apparently had no intention of preventing the police from doing so.

5. *The SCCRC recognised that Tony Gauci was not motivated by money and that he had allegedly been made an offer to go to Tripoli and be rewarded 'by Libyan Government officials'.*

This misrepresents the SCCRC's findings. What the commission actually said was: 'Mr Gauci may well have given entirely credible evidence, notwithstanding an alleged interest in financial payment. On the other hand there are sound reasons to believe that the information in question would have been used by the defence as a means of challenging his credibility. Such a challenge may well have been justified, and in the Commission's view was capable of affecting the course of the evidence and the eventual outcome of the trial.'

With regard to the differing accounts by Megrahi the Commission noted that:

i. *There were inconsistencies and differences in account between his statements to an investigative journalist, his defence team and the SCCRC in matters of significance.*

Inconsistencies in statements do not prove guilt. There were numerous inconsistencies in the statements of the Crown's star witness, Tony Gauci. Like Gauci, Megrahi recounted his story many times, always under conditions of great stress. It is therefore hardly surprising that there were some inconsistencies between his statements.

ii. *He had 'personal relationships' with various members of the Libyan intelligence services, including Senussi and accepted that he had been seconded to the Libyan intelligence services (JSO) and that Said Rashid was his superior in the JSO.*

Megrahi freely revealed these connections to his lawyers, to the SCCRC and in *Megrahi: You Are My Jury.* He would also have been happy to testify about them at trial. It is not a crime to be related to members of the intelligence services.

iii. *Senussi was involved in his secondment to Libyan intelligence services (JSO).*

It is also not a crime to be a member of the intelligence services. Furthermore, the only evidence that Megrahi was a senior intelligence agent was the testimony of the discredited CIA informant Majid Giaka, who also claimed, on the record, that Colonel Gadafy was a freemason.

iv. *He had travelled with a Colonel in the Libyan intelligence services (JSO) on a false passport in 1987.*

Megrahi had a reasonable explanation for his false passport. The fact that he travelled with an intelligence services officer did not mean that he was himself an intelligence officer and less still that he was a terrorist.

v. *Megrahi gave the Commission conflicting accounts of his connection to the Libyan intelligence services (JSO).*

Megrahi consistently said that he was seconded to the intelligence service, the JSO, for one year. He was also open about the fact that he was related to some senior intelligence officers.

vi. *Megrahi confirmed he had knowledge of a man in Spain who was assassinated because he was allegedly an American spy.*

This is a reference to a pre-trial precognition statement, in which Megrahi said: 'I remember that there was a man in Spain who used to send back articles from the Spanish media. Sometime during the 1990s it turned out that he was an American spy and he was assassinated.' Doubtless many other people, including Spaniards, knew of the incident, which was entirely irrelevant to Megrahi's case.

vii. *Megrahi has given a number of different explanations to his lawyers and the Commission about his presence in Malta and use of a false passport on 21 December 1988.*

Megrahi said that he regularly used his false passport for a number of reasons. The fact that he could not remember the precise reason why he used it on 21 December 1988 is not surprising given that, according to him, the trip was fairly routine. If he wanted to lie, it would have been easier to stick to one story.

viii. *The SCCRC believed 'there was a real risk that the trial court would have viewed his explanations . . . as weak or unconvincing'* *'In particular, the Commission notes the unsatisfactory nature of aspects of their [Megrahi and Fhimah] explanations and the various contradictions which are apparent both within and between their accounts. Although it is possible there are innocent reasons for these deficiencies, they do lead the Commission to have reservations about the credibility and reliability of both as witnesses.'*

As the Crown Office well knew, inconsistencies are not proof of guilt. It also failed to point out that the commission concluded in the next paragraph, 'It cannot be said, however, that the applicant's accounts amount to a confession of guilt.'

Notes on the Text

1 Flawed Charges

1. Bedford statement S1548A; Sidhu statement S967G; Sahota statement S2139.
2. Tony Gauci statement S4677.
3. Tony Gauci statement S4677F.
4. Scottish Home and Health Department Guidelines on the Conduct of Identification Parades, May 1982.
5. Bell statement S2632AR.
6. *Sunday Times*, 23 October 2005.
7. Marquise, Richard, *Scotbom: Evidence and the Lockerbie Investigation*. New York: Algora, 2006, P.102.
8. FBI report on Giaka interviews, 14 July 1991, police reference DE121, Crown production 1486.
9. Marquise, *Scotbom*.
10. FBI report on Giaka interviews, 27 July to 1 August 1991, police reference DE122, Crown production 1487.
11. FBI report of Giaka interview, 8 August 1991.
12. Ralf Schaefer BKA statement, 9 March 1999, and deposition in Pan Am civil trial, 17 January 1992.
13. McAteer statement S3743A.
14. Ramp progress sheet, police reference DC625, Crown production 939; Load plan, police reference DC626, Crown production 940.
15. Camilleri statement S4910.
16. Darmanin statement S5019A.
17. Wilfred Borg statement S5045E.
18. Report by DCI Bell on April 1989 explosive tests 1 to 5 at Indian Head, police reference D4198.
19. Hayes notes, 26 January 1989, police reference PT/90, Crown production 1497.
20. Bedford statement S1548A.
21. May Inquiry interim and final reports.
22. R v Ward [1993] 1 WLR 619, 96 Cr App Rep 1.
23. Appeal judgment in the case of John Berry, 28 September 1993.
24. Allen Feraday trial evidence in the case of R v Assali.
25. CCRC Statement of Reasons in the case of Hassan Assali.
26. Entwistle statement S450U.
27. Entwistle SCCRC interview, 24 June 2005; Brown SCCRC interview 26 September 2005.
28. Hayes SCCRC interview, 8 March 2006.

29. Vincent Vassallo's diary, police reference DC1149, Crown production 531.

30. Thatcher, Margaret, *The Downing Street Years*. London: Harper Collins, 1993.

2 Getting Away with Murder

1. 'Bush: Iran Must Share Blame in Jet Downing' *Chicago Tribune*, 15 July 1988.

2. Evans, Lt Col David, U.S. Marine Corps (Retired), *Vincennes: A Case Study*, US Naval Institute, Proceedings Magazine, August 1993 Vol. 119/8/1,086

3. Cooley, John, *Payback: America's Long War in the Middle East*. New York: Brassey's, 1992.

4. Matthew Cox and Tom Foster, *Their Darkest Day: The Tragedy of Pan Am 103 and Its Legacy of Hope*. New York: Grove Weidenfeld, 1992, p. 19.

5. Katz, *Israel Versus Jibril*, chapter 11; Emerson, Steven and Duffy, Brian, *The Fall of Pan Am 103: Inside the Lockerbie Investigation*. New York: G P Putnam's Sons, 1990, chapter 14.

6. Baer, Robert, *See No Evil: The True Story of a Ground Soldier in the CIA's War on Terrorism*. New York: Crown, 2002.

7. Author's note of meetings with Robert Baer, 9 and 10 February 2002.

8. BKA memo, 13 February 1989.

9. BKA report: *Terrorist activities of the Popular Front for the Liberation of Palestine, General Command, in the Federal Republic of Germany*, 27 October 1988.

10. FBI FD302 report of interview of Marwan Khreesat.

11. Ghadanfar BKA interview, 26 October 1988.

12. BKA inventory of items seized from 28 Sandweg, Frankfurt, police reference DW198, Crown production 1672; BKA photos of 28 Sandweg, police reference DW166, Crown production 1637.

13. BKA letter to Frankfurt Public Prosecutor, 17 March 1989; Judicial interview of Khadorah, 6 July 1989; Dalkamoni BKA interview, 13 January 1989.

14. DCI Harry Bell memo to SIO John Orr, 14 July 1989.

15. Notebook of DC William Grant, police reference AZ/68, Crown Production 124; DC James Barclay statement S453B; Barclay trial evidence, 8 May 2000, trial transcript p.690.

16. LPS form 1, police reference DP/28, Crown Production 288; RARDE scientists' examination notes.

17. Crown Office letter to Taylor & Kelly Solicitors, 1 September 2008.

18. Hashem Abassi interview, 14 April 1989, police reference D4039.

19. Marwan Khreesat, defence precognition statement, 22 June 2000.
20. FBI FD302 report of interview with Marwan Khreesat.
21. Translation of the Goben memorandum.
22. Author's note of meetings with Robert Baer, 9 and 10 February 2002.
23. Emerson and Duffy, *The Fall of Pan Am 103*.
24. Report of the President's Commission on Aviation Security and Terrorism. US Government Printing Office, 1990.
25. ABC Television interview, 30 November 1989.
26. Washington Times, 30 December 1988.
27. *Daily Express*, 31 December 1988.
28. Author interviews with police officer.
29. Emerson and Duffy, *The Fall of Pan Am 103*; *Private Eye*, 8 May 1992.
30. Author interview with dog handler.
31. *Sunday Times*, 16 April 1989.
32. Siddiqi statement S3135B.
33. Nazir Jaafar interview, *Mail on Sunday*, 1 January 1989.
34. Pan Am leaflet found in luggage of Khaled Jaafar, police reference PD1043-10R, Crown production 197; BKA memo, 21 April 1989, BKA investigative file VI-7.
35. List of Jaafar baggage contents attached to memo from FBI West German Legal Attache David Barham to BKA, 7 April 1989.
36. The 'Goben memorandum'.
37. 'Rabbieh' defence precognition statement.
38. Scottish police summary of Talb investigations,9 January 1991, police reference D6921.
39. Abdul Salem Abu Nada statement, 9 July 1990.
40. Talb Scottish police interview, 3 April 1990, police reference D6023.
41. Tony Gauci statement S4677K.
42. Bell statement S2632E.
43. Dr Drago Dragavac Crown precognition statement.
44. Police document *Summary of Swedish Investigations*, 9 January 1991, police reference D6921.
45. Abu Talb police interview, 3 to 5 April 1990, police reference D6023; schedule of clothing confiscated from Abu Talb's house, prepared by DC Callum Entwistle.
46. Bollier interview by BKA and Frankfurt prosecutor, 6 October 1993.
47. Dalkamoni BKA interview, 24 April 1989.
48. Wenzel BKA interviews.

3 A Nation Condemned

1. US and UK governments' joint declaration A/46/827 S/23308, 27 November 1991.
2. Matar, Khalil I. and Thabit, Robert W. *Lockerbie and Libya: A Study in International Relations*. Jefferson: McFardland & Co., 2004.
3. UN Security Council resolution 731.
4. UN Security Council resolution 748.
5. Scharf, Michael P., *The Lockerbie Model*, chapter in Bassiouni, Cherif ed., *International Criminal Law*, 3rd edition. Transnational: Brill, 2007.
6. UN Security Council resolution 833.
7. International Court of Justice Application, 3 March 1992.
8. *'Nelson Mandela breaks impasse on Lockerbie duo'*, Inter Press Service 28 October 1997.
9. Matar, Khalil I. and Thabit, Robert W., *Lockerbie and Libya: A Study in International Relations*. Jefferson: McFardland & Co., 2004.
10. Summary of ICJ judgment, 27 February 1998.
11. Niblock, Tim, *'Pariah States' and Sanctions in the Middle East*. Boulder: Lynne Rienner Publishers Inc, 2002.
12. UN Document S/1998/201.
13. Niblock, Tim, *'Pariah States' and Sanctions in the Middle East*. Boulder: Lynne Rienner Publishers Inc, 2002.
14. UN Document S/1998/201.
15. Letter from Chargé d'Affaires a.i. of the Permanent Mission of the Libyan Arab Jamahiriya to the President of the UN Security Council, 15 August 2003.
16. Shukri Ghanem interview, BBC Radio 4 *Today* programme, 24 February 2004. Transcript available on BBC website at *http://news.bbc. co.uk/1/hi/uk_politics/3517101.stm*.
17. Saif al-Islam Gadafy interview, BBC TV *Conspiracy Files* documentary, 29 August 2008.
18. *The Herald*, 12 November 2006.
19. Michael Scharf interview, BBC TV *Conspiracy Files* documentary, 29 August 2008.
20. *'How the Lockerbie Trial Paid off for U.S. Security Interests'*, article by Michael Scharf, *Boston Globe*, 10 February 2001.

4 A Shameful Verdict

1. Tony Gauci statement S4677R.
2. Identity parade report police reference DN33, Crown production 1324.
3. Tony Gauci trial evidence, 11 July 2000, trial transcript page 4774 to 4778.

4. Tony Gauci trial evidence, 11 July 2000, trial transcript page 4739.
5. Tony Gauci trial evidence, 11 July 2000, trial transcript page 4821.
6. Giaka trial evidence, 28 September 2000, trial transcript pages 6979-81.
7. Alastair Campbell QC final submissions, 10 January 2001, trial transcript page 9504.

5 Burying the Evidence

1. Stauton defence precognition statement.
2. Norman McFadyen letter to Eddie MacKechnie, 2 January 2000.
3. Bill Taylor QC, 22 August 2000, trial transcript pages 6087 to 6091.
4. The Lord Advocate Colin Boyd QC, 22 August 2000, trial transcript pages 6093 to 6101.
5. Non-disclosure agreement June 2000.
6. Richard Keen QC, 25 August 2000, trial transcript page 6522.
7. The Lord Advocate Colin Boyd QC, 21 September 2000, trial transcript pages 6696 to 6695.
8. CIA cables released by Crown, 20 and 21 September 2000.
9. Bill Taylor QC, 21 September 2000, trial transcript page 6723.
10. Memo by Norman McFadyen to Alastair Campbell QC and Alan Turnbull QC, 2 June 2000.
11. Partially redacted CIA cables, 25 August 2000 version, Crown productions 804 to 828.
12. *Daily Mirror*, 11 September 2001.
13. Tony Gauci defence precognition statement, 8 October 1999.
14. SCCRC Statement of Reasons, para. 24.108.
15. SCCRC Statement of Reasons, para. 22.64
16. SCCRC Statement of Reasons, para. 22.31.
17. Tony Gauci SCCRC interview, 2 and 3 August 2006.
18. Paul Gauci SCCRC interview, 2 and 3 August 2006.
19. SCCRC Statement of Reasons, para. 22.67.
20. SCCRC Statement of Reasons, para. 22.84.
21. Bell diary extract, 28 September 1989.
22. Bell memo to Gilchrist, 21 February 1991.
23. Strathclyde police report, 10 June 1999.
24. *Impact Assessment Anthony Gauci Paul Gauci*, 12 January 2001.
25. *Anthony and Paul Gauci Reward Compensation Payments*, undated report.
26. SIO McCulloch letter to US Embassy in The Hague, 7 February 2001.
27. SIO McCulloch letter to US Department of Justice, 19 April 2002.
28. SCCRC Statement of Reasons, para. 23.19.
29. Tony Gauci trial evidence, 11 July 2000, trial transcript page 4752.

30. Tony Gauci trial evidence, 11 July 2000, trial transcript page 4753.
31. SCCRC Statement of Reasons, para. 23.59.
32. Tony Gauci SCCRC interview, 2 and 3 August 2006.
33. SCCRC Statement of Reasons, para. 25.1 to 25.8.
34. SCCRC Statement of Reasons, para. 26.14.
35. SCCRC Statement of Reasons, para. 26.18.
36. SCCRC Statement of Reasons, para. 26.20.
37. SCCRC Statement of Reasons, para. 26.22.
38. Memo by Detective Constable Entwistle, 3 April 1990 police reference D8925.
39. Hayes trial evidence, 7 June 2000, trial transcript pages 2681 to 2684.
40. Feraday Crown precognition statement, 2 December 1999.
41. Feraday Crown precognition statement, 30 March 2000.
42. Lawrence Whittaker trial evidence, 5 December 2000, trial transcript 9329 to 9435.
43. McAteer statement S3743A.
44. Dr Rosemary Wilkinson statement S5579A.
45. Urs Bonfadelli affidavit, 1 April 2009.
46. Report of Dr Jess Cawley, 11 May 2009.
47. Report of Dr Chris McArdle.

6 A Bigger Picture

1. Melvin Goodman interview in *The Power of Nightmares*, BBC documentary series, Episode 1, broadcast 20 October 2004.
2. Sterling, Claire, *The Terror Network*. New York: Holt, Rinehart and Winston, 1981.
3. Martin, David and Walcott, John, *Best Laid Plans: The Inside Story of America's War against Terrorism*. New York: Harper & Row, 1988.
4. Perry, Mark, *Eclipse: The Last Days of the CIA*. New York: William Morrow & Co., 1992.
5. Yallop, David, *To the Ends of the Earth: The Hunt for the Jackal*. London: Jonathan Cape, 1993.
6. Biography provided to the Senate Democratic Policy Committee Hearing: *National Security Implications of Disclosing the Identity of an Intelligence Operative*, 24 October 2003.
7. Cannistraro interview for *American Radio Works* documentary *Shadow over Lockerbie*.
8. *Washington Post*, 2 October 1986.
9. Claim was reported by the British High Commission in Canberra, Australia, in a press release dated 16 May 1995.

10. Author interview with Scottish mountain rescue team members, 26 November 2001.
11. Author interview with military helicopter crew member.
12. Tam Dalyell interview, *The Maltese Double Cross* documentary.
13. Author non-attributable interviews with various search volunteers.
14. Innes Graham interview, *The Maltese Double Cross* documentary.
15. Author non-attributable interview with witness.
16. Author non-attributable interviews with police officer.
17. Volunteer searcher interviewed by author.
18. Tony Lloyd MP, Minister of State, Foreign and Commonwealth Office, House of Commons debate 11 June 1997.
19. Author non-attributable interviews with Scottish and English mountain rescue team members.
20. Written answer by Scottish Office Minister Lord James Douglas-Hamilton, 6 March 1995.
21. Johnson, David, *Lockerbie: The Real Story*. London: Bloomsbury, 1989.
22. Williamson, SCCRC interview 2 April 2007.
23. Baird, Crown precognition statement.
24. SCCRC Statement of Reasons, paragraphs 12.41 to 12.61.
25. David Johnston interview, *The Maltese Double Cross* documentary.
26. Tiny Rowland statement, 14 August 1994.
27. Tam Dalyell MP interview with author; Todd Leventhal letter to Tam Dalyell MP, 28 April 1995
28. Letter from Michael O'Brien, US Embassy, London, to UK press with enclosures, 9 May 1995; press release with enclosures issued by Scottish Crown Office, 10 May 1995.
29. Press release with enclosures issued by British High Commission, Canberra, 16 May 1995.
30. Fax from First Secretary (Information & Internal), British High Commission, Canberra to Foreign & Commonwealth Office, Drugs, International Crime and Terrorism Department, 25 May 1995.
31. *Washington Post*, 11 January 1990.
32. Cecil Parkinson, unbroadcast extract of interview for Channel 4 *Dispatches* programme on the *Marchioness* disaster, 1995.
33. Interview with Martin Cadman in the *Maltese Double Cross* documentary.

7 The Crown out of Control

1. Crown answers to petition for access to forensic materials, 20 February 2009.
2. Crown letter to Taylor & Kelly, 12 December 2008.

3. Taylor & Kelly letter to Crown Office, 20 January 2009.
4. Crown Office statement, 23 March 2012.
5. *Daily Record*, 24 March 2012.
6. Crown Office statement to BBC Radio Scotland *Newsdrive* programme, 14 March 2012.
7. Statement by the Lord Advocate Frank Mulholland QC, 1 March 2013 http://www.crownoffice.gov.uk/News/Releases/2013/03/Lockerbie-investigators-visit-Libya.
8. Translated extract of *Expressen* article on Aljazeera English website, 23 February 2011.
9. *Sunday Times*, 27 February 2011.
10. BBC *Newsnight*, 1 April 2011.
11. Text accompanying Younes statement, BBC News website, 25 February 2011; BBC interview with General Abdel Fattah Younes Al-Abidi, BBC News website, 25 February 2011.
12. Article by John Simpson, BBC News website, 25 February 2011.
13. english.peopledaily.com.cn/200402/25/eng20040225_135801.shtml
14. *Daily Telegraph*, 18 July 2011.
15. ITV *Tonight* programme, broadcast 19 January 2012.
16. Ashur Shamis interview, *Spotlight on Terror*, vol. 3, issue 3, 24 March 2005.
17. *Wall Street Journal*, 30 August 2011.
18. *The Times*, 29 August 2011.
19. *Daily Telegraph*, 1 March 2013.
20. Crown Office press release, 1 March 2013.
21. Justice for Megrahi committee letter to Kenny MacAskill, 13 September 2012.
22. Lord Advocate letter to James Kelly MSP, 29 January 2013.

8 A Failure of Politics

1. Scottish Criminal Cases Review Commission (Permitted Disclosure of Information) Order 2009.
2. Parliamentary answer by justice secretary Kenny MacAskill, 11 January 2011.
3. Scottish government spokesman quoted in the *Herald*, 21 May 2012.
4. John Ashton email to the Scottish government, 25 September 2012.
5. Letter from Patrick Down, Scottish government justice directorate, law reform division to John Ashton.
6. John Ashton email to the Scottish government, 19 November 2012.
7. Letter from Scottish government justice directorate to Robert Forrester, secretary of Justice for Megrahi, 14 September 2010.

8. Scottish government letter to Scottish parliament's public petitions committee, 7 January 2011.

9. Kenny MacAskill letter to Scottish parliament's justice committee, 24 June 2013.

10. The *Herald*, 5 October 2012.

11. Scottish Liberal Democrats statement, 24 May 2012. http://scotlib-dems.org.uk/news/2012/05/rennie-calls-public-inquiry-over-lockerbie

12. The *Herald*, 1 June 2011.

13. The *Herald*, 31 May 2011.

14. The *Guardian*, 1 June 2011.

15. *Holyrood* magazine interview with Alex Salmond, 13 June 2011.

16. *Sunday Herald*, 20 November 2011.

17. Author interview with Abdelbaset al-Megrahi.

18. Kenny MacAskill statement to the Scottish Parliament, 29 February 2012.

19. *The Herald*, 6 August 2009.

Conclusion: A System in Denial

1. McKie, Iain and Russell, Michael, *Shirley McKie: The Price of Innocence*. Edinburgh: Birlinn, 2007.

2. BBC News website, 4 March 2006.

Appendix 2

1. *Scotland on Sunday*, 18 March 2012.

Index

Note: Arabic names. In accordance with normal convention, Arabic
personal names prefixed with Al or El have been indexed under the main
part of the surname, e.g. Abdelbaset Al-Megrahi is indexed under Megrahi.
However, corporate bodies and places have been indexed under the prefix,
e.g. El Al airline is under El.